KT-569-158

CAMBRIDGE SCHOOL

# *Shakespeare*

# Romeo

## AND

# Juliet

Edited by Rex Gibson

Series Editor: Rex Gibson
Director, Shakespeare and Schools Project

CAMBRIDGE
UNIVERSITY PRESS

PUBLISHED BY THE PRESS SYNDICATE OF THE UNIVERSITY OF CAMBRIDGE
The Pitt Building, Trumpington Street, Cambridge CB2 1RP, United Kingdom

CAMBRIDGE UNIVERSITY PRESS
The Edinburgh Building, Cambridge CB2 2RU, United Kingdom
40 West 20th Street, New York, NY 10011–4211, USA
10 Stamford Road, Oakleigh, Melbourne 3166, Australia

© Commentary and notes Cambridge University Press 1992
© Text Cambridge University Press 1984

This book is in copyright. Subject to statutory exception
and to the provisions of relevant collective licensing agreements,
no reproduction of any part may take place without
the written permission of Cambridge University Press.

First published 1992
Eighth printing 1997

Printed in the United Kingdom at the University Press, Cambridge

*A catalogue record for this book is available from the British Library*

*Library of Congress Cataloguing in Publication data applied for*

ISBN 0 521 39574 7


Designed by Richard Morris
Illustrations by Jones and Sewell Associates and Hemesh Alles
Picture research by Callie Kendall

*Thanks are due to the following for permission to reproduce photographs:*

p. 6, © 1961 Beta Productions. Renewed 1989 United Artists Pictures, Inc. All rights
reserved; p. 16, reproduced by permission of the Trustees of the Victoria & Albert Museum;
pp. 22, 50, Mansell Collection; pp. 24, 58, 64, 82, Angus McBean; p. 38, Nobby Clark;
p. 60, Mary Evans Picture Library; p. 70, by permission of the Houghton Library, Harvard
University; from Saint-Didier's treatise on swordplay, reproduced by permission of the
Syndics of Cambridge University Library; p. 90*l*, *Romeo and Juliet*, © 1991 Paramount
Pictures; p. 90*r*, Joe Cocks Studio; pp. 100, 124, 148, John Hayes/photographs by
Shakespeare Centre Library, Stratford-upon-Avon; p. 108, Ivan Kynel; p. 110, Topham
Picture Source; pp. 124, 169, Harvard Theatre Collection; p. 140, Shakespeare Centre
Library, Stratford-upon-Avon/photo by Gordon Goode.

Jacket: Joe Cocks Studio

# Contents

# Cambridge School Shakespeare

This edition of *Romeo and Juliet* is part of the *Cambridge School Shakespeare* series. Like every other play in the series, it has been specially prepared to help all students in schools and colleges.

This *Romeo and Juliet* aims to be different from other editions of the play. It invites you to bring the play to life in your classroom, hall or drama studio through enjoyable activities that will increase your understanding. Actors have created their different interpretations of the play over the centuries. Similarly, you are encouraged to make up your own mind about *Romeo and Juliet*, rather than having someone else's interpretation handed down to you.

*Cambridge School Shakespeare* does not offer you a cut-down or simplified version of the play. This is Shakespeare's language, filled with imaginative possibilities. You will find on every left-hand page: a summary of the action, an explanation of unfamiliar words, a choice of activities on Shakespeare's language, characters and stories.

Between each act and in the pages at the end of the play, you will find notes, illustrations and activities. These will help to increase your understanding of the whole play.

There are a large number of activities to give you the widest choice to suit your own particular needs. Please don't think you have to do every one. Choose the activities that will help you most.

This edition will be of value to you whether you are studying for an examination, reading for pleasure, or thinking of putting on the play to entertain others. You can work on the activities on your own or in groups. Many of the activities suggest a particular group size, but don't be afraid to make up larger or smaller groups to suit your own purposes.

Although you are invited to treat *Romeo and Juliet* as a play, you don't need special dramatic or theatrical skills to do the activities. By choosing your activities, and by exploring and experimenting, you can make your own interpretations of Shakespeare's language, characters and stories. Whatever you do, remember that Shakespeare wrote his plays to be acted, watched and enjoyed.

Rex Gibson

This edition of *Romeo and Juliet* uses the text of the play established by G. Blakemore Evans in *The New Cambridge Shakespeare*.

# List of characters

The Play is set in Verona and Mantua

*The Chorus gives a preview of the play: the bitter quarrels of the Montagues and Capulets are ended only by the death of their children, Romeo and Juliet.*

---

### 1  What began the feud? (in groups of three or four)

But *why* were the Montagues and Capulets such bitter enemies? Shakespeare never tells us and no one really knows. Talk together about why you think these two families should have been at each others' throats for so long. Prepare a short scene to show what long-ago incident ('ancient grudge') sparked off the hatred between two of Verona's leading families. Present your scene to the class.

### 2  The whole play (in groups of five to eight)

The Prologue gives an outline of the play. Work out your own short play to show all the action described. One person reads the Prologue aloud, a line at a time. The others mime what is described in each line. Each group shows its Prologue in turn.

### 3  Vital words

Pick out two or three words or phrases from the Prologue that you feel are powerful or imaginative. Compare 'your' words with the ones chosen by two or three other students. Talk together about why you think 'your' words are vital. As you read through the play, add other key words to your list.

### 4  Write your own sonnet!

The Prologue is in the form of a **sonnet** (fourteen lines). There are several sonnets in *Romeo and Juliet*. Turn to page 211 to learn more about sonnets, and try your hand at writing one.

# The tragedy of Romeo and Juliet

## THE PROLOGUE

*Enter* CHORUS.

Two households, both alike in dignity,
In fair Verona (where we lay our scene),
From ancient grudge break to new mutiny,
Where civil blood makes civil hands unclean.
From forth the fatal loins of these two foes            5
A pair of star-crossed lovers take their life;
Whose misadventured piteous overthrows
Doth with their death bury their parents' strife.
The fearful passage of their death-marked love,
And the continuance of their parents' rage,            10
Which but their children's end nought could remove,
Is now the two hours' traffic of our stage;
The which if you with patient ears attend,
What here shall miss, our toil shall strive to mend.    *[Exit]*

*Capulet's servants, Sampson and Gregory, joke together and boast that they are superior to the Montagues. Suddenly two of Montague's servants appear. What will happen?*

## 1 Bully boys . . .? (in pairs – one as Gregory, one as Sampson)

Read this page of conversation aloud together several times, changing roles.

Talk about these two characters. Are they really as brave as they brag they are?

## 2 'Take the wall . . . goes to the wall' (in pairs)

Have a close look at the two uses of 'wall' in lines 10–13. Show, using your bodies and a classroom wall, what you think one or both of these expressions could mean.

## 3 What do you think?

Here's what one student wrote about Sampson and Gregory:

'Times never change! Like typical men these boneheads boast about their sexual prowess and turn everything into a sex-joke ('stand', 'thrust', 'maidenheads', 'tool', 'weapon'). Why on earth did Shakespeare put such crude characters and language into a play that's about love, not sex?'

What would you say in answer to her question?

## 4 Scene Locations

At the beginning of each scene, a location is given (for example, 'Verona A public place'). But no one can be sure of the precise location Shakespeare had in mind. So, as you read through the play, don't be afraid to suggest, with reasons, alternative places where each scene could be set.

---

**bucklers** small round shields
**choler** anger
**poor-John** dried hake, cheap food that Elizabethans linked with lack of sex-drive

**two servingmen** in modern productions the second servant is usually Peter

# ACT 1   SCENE 1
## Verona   A public place

Enter SAMPSON and GREGORY, with swords and bucklers.

SAMPSON  Gregory, on my word, we'll not carry coals.

GREGORY  No, for then we should be colliers.

SAMPSON  I mean, and we be in choler, we'll draw.

GREGORY  Ay, while you live, draw your neck out of collar.

SAMPSON  I strike quickly, being moved.                                        5

GREGORY  But thou art not quickly moved to strike.

SAMPSON  A dog of the house of Montague moves me.

GREGORY  To move is to stir, and to be valiant is to stand: therefore
if thou art moved thou runn'st away.

SAMPSON  A dog of that house shall move me to stand: I will take the    10
wall of any man or maid of Montague's.

GREGORY  That shows thee a weak slave, for the weakest goes to the
wall.

SAMPSON  'Tis true, and therefore women being the weaker vessels are
ever thrust to the wall: therefore I will push Montague's men from    15
the wall, and thrust his maids to the wall.

GREGORY  The quarrel is between our masters, and us their men.

SAMPSON  'Tis all one, I will show myself a tyrant: when I have fought
with the men, I will be civil with the maids; I will cut off their
heads.                                                                  20

GREGORY  The heads of the maids?

SAMPSON  Ay, the heads of the maids, or their maidenheads, take it in
what sense thou wilt.

GREGORY  They must take it in sense that feel it.

SAMPSON  Me they shall feel while I am able to stand, and 'tis known    25
I am a pretty piece of flesh.

GREGORY  'Tis well thou art not fish; if thou hadst, thou hadst been
poor-John. Draw thy tool, here comes of the house of Montagues.

*Enter two other* SERVINGMEN, [*one being* ABRAM].

SAMPSON  My naked weapon is out. Quarrel, I will back thee.

GREGORY  How, turn thy back and run?                                    30

*Sampson and Gregory begin a quarrel with the Montagues. Benvolio (a Montague) tries to make peace, but Tybalt (a Capulet) adds flames to the fire, seizing the opportunity to fight.*

## 1 Setting the play (in groups of four or five)

The American musical film *West Side Story* was based on *Romeo and Juliet*. It was set in modern New York, with the lovers belonging to opposing gangs, the Jets and the Sharks. Some stage versions also use modern locations, such as Belfast and Beirut.

Talk together about other possible settings where the quarrels (that Shakespeare set in Verona) could take place. Decide which location you prefer. When you present your group's suggestion to the class, make sure you can give several reasons for your setting.

## 2 Tybalt – what's he like? (in groups of three or four)

Tybalt speaks only five lines, (lines 57–8 and lines 61–3) but they tell us a great deal about him. Choose one word from each line and work out a short mime using those five words to show Tybalt's character. When each group has shown its mime, talk together about how much agreement exists on what Tybalt is like.

**bite my thumb** a rude gesture in Elizabethan times. What are similar provocative gestures today?
**washing** slashing

**hinds** young female deer. Tybalt is punning on 'heart' (hart = male deer), mocking Benvolio for fighting with servants (see page 213)

SAMPSON Fear me not.

GREGORY No, marry, I fear thee!

SAMPSON Let us take the law of our sides, let them begin.

GREGORY I will frown as I pass by, and let them take it as they list.

SAMPSON Nay, as they dare. I will bite my thumb at them, which is    35
disgrace to them if they bear it.

ABRAM Do you bite your thumb at us, sir?

SAMPSON I do bite my thumb, sir.

ABRAM Do you bite your thumb at us, sir?

SAMPSON [*Aside to Gregory*] Is the law of our side if I say ay?    40

GREGORY [*Aside to Sampson*] No.

SAMPSON No, sir, I do not bite my thumb at you, sir, but I bite my
thumb, sir.

GREGORY Do you quarrel, sir?

ABRAM Quarrel, sir? No, sir.    45

SAMPSON But if you do, sir, I am for you. I serve as good a man as
you.

ABRAM No better.

SAMPSON Well, sir.

*Enter* BENVOLIO.

GREGORY [*Aside to Sampson*] Say 'better', here comes one of my    50
master's kinsmen.

SAMPSON Yes, better, sir.

ABRAM You lie.

SAMPSON Draw, if you be men. Gregory, remember thy washing blow.

*They fight.*

BENVOLIO Part, fools!    55
Put up your swords, you know not what you do.
[*Beats down their swords.*]

*Enter* TYBALT.

TYBALT What, art thou drawn among these heartless hinds?
Turn thee, Benvolio, look upon thy death.

BENVOLIO I do but keep the peace. Put up thy sword,
Or manage it to part these men with me.    60

TYBALT What, drawn and talk of peace? I hate the word,
As I hate hell, all Montagues, and thee.
Have at thee, coward.
[*They fight.*]

*A furious riot develops. Capulet and Montague join in. Prince Escales, angry
and exasperated, stops the fight. He rebukes Montague and Capulet.*

---

### 1  A snapshot at the height of the riot
(in groups of eleven or more)

Everyone takes a part. There are at least eleven speaking characters
so far. You can add as many other servants and officers as you wish.
Use the hall or drama studio if you can, but it will work well in the
classroom if you clear some space.

Each group prepares and presents a snapshot photograph (a
'tableau' or 'frozen moment') showing the height of the riot at line 72,
'Rebellious subjects, enemies to peace'.

Your group 'snapshot' shows precisely what each character is doing
at *that* moment. This means thinking carefully about what *your*
character has said so far, then 'freezing' as that person at this moment
in the riot. Remember, each character is doing something in relation
to *other* characters, so try to show those relationships. It takes time to
think out, experiment, and then present the most dramatic picture.

Hold your 'freeze' for at least sixty seconds – no movement
whatever. The other groups watch for that time. They identify exactly
who is who. If your preparation is well done, the audience ought to be
able to identify every character with 100 per cent success!

### 2  The Prince's speech (in groups of four)

Read the speech aloud, each person reading one line only, then
handing on to the next. Read it again around the group, but this time,
when your turn comes, say only *one* word from each of your lines (the
word you think is most important). Do this three or four times, with a
different person beginning the speech each time. Talk together about
the words chosen and the tone in which you think the Prince speaks.

---

**clubs, bills, and
partisans** weapons: bills are long-
handled pikes, partisans are long,
broad-headed spears
**train** attendants to the Prince

**profaners** abusers (because they
stain their swords with neighbours'
blood)
**cast by** throw aside

*Enter [several of both houses, who join the fray, and] three or four*
*Citizens [as* OFFICERS *of the Watch,] with clubs or partisans.*

OFFICERS  Clubs, bills, and partisans! Strike! Beat them down!
    Down with the Capulets! Down with the Montagues!          65

*Enter old* CAPULET *in his gown, and his wife* [LADY CAPULET].

CAPULET  What noise is this? Give me my long sword, ho!
LADY CAPULET  A crutch, a crutch! why call you for a sword?
CAPULET  My sword, I say! old Montague is come,
    And flourishes his blade in spite of me.

*Enter old* MONTAGUE *and his wife* [LADY MONTAGUE].

MONTAGUE  Thou villain Capulet! – Hold me not, let me go.          70
LADY MONTAGUE  Thou shalt not stir one foot to seek a foe.

*Enter* PRINCE ESCALES *with his train.*

PRINCE  Rebellious subjects, enemies to peace,
    Profaners of this neighbour-stainèd steel –
    Will they not hear? – What ho, you men, you beasts!
    That quench the fire of your pernicious rage          75
    With purple fountains issuing from your veins:
    On pain of torture, from those bloody hands
    Throw your mistempered weapons to the ground,
    And hear the sentence of your movèd prince.
    Three civil brawls, bred of an airy word,          80
    By thee, old Capulet, and Montague,
    Have thrice disturbed the quiet of our streets,
    And made Verona's ancient citizens
    Cast by their grave beseeming ornaments
    To wield old partisans, in hands as old,          85
    Cankered with peace, to part your cankered hate;
    If ever you disturb our streets again,
    Your lives shall pay the forfeit of the peace.
    For this time all the rest depart away:
    You, Capulet, shall go along with me,          90
    And, Montague, come you this afternoon,
    To know our farther pleasure in this case,
    To old Free-town, our common judgement-place.
    Once more, on pain of death, all men depart.
        *Exeunt [all but Montague, Lady Montague, and Benvolio]*

*Benvolio recounts the story of the riot. He tells Lady Montague how Romeo has avoided meeting him. Montague confirms that Romeo has been keeping to himself, preferring night to day.*

## 1 Show Benvolio's story of the riot
(in groups of four to seven)

Take each moment in the developing fight as Benvolio tells it ('Here . . . adversary'; 'And . . . approach'; 'I . . . them'; 'in . . . prepared', etc.). Present a slow-motion version and a fast-motion version of the story, showing each action described in lines 97–106.

You could appoint a narrator, but you may decide that there's no need for someone to actually speak the words.

As you watch other groups presenting their mimes, see if they perform every incident that Benvolio mentions. You'll have to watch the fast-motion versions very carefully!

## 2 What's the matter with Romeo?
(in pairs – as Benvolio and Montague)

Read aloud lines 109–31 several times, changing characters. Talk together about Romeo's behaviour as described in the speeches. Why is he behaving like this? Suggest a number of possible reasons.

## 3 A change in style of speaking? (in pairs)

The language of Benvolio and Montague (lines 109–31) is different from the style of all the other language used in the play so far. Identify one or two of the differences.

Some students find these two speeches rather static after all the action that has gone before in this opening scene. If you were directing the play, what would be your advice to the actors playing Benvolio and Montague on how to speak their lines?

---

**Aurora** Greek goddess of dawn
**portentous** ominous
**humour** mood

MONTAGUE  Who set this ancient quarrel new abroach?                    95
       Speak, nephew, were you by when it began?
BENVOLIO  Here were the servants of your adversary,
       And yours, close fighting ere I did approach:
       I drew to part them; in the instant came
       The fiery Tybalt, with his sword prepared,                    100
       Which, as he breathed defiance to my ears,
       He swung about his head and cut the winds,
       Who, nothing hurt withal, hissed him in scorn;
       While we were interchanging thrusts and blows,
       Came more and more, and fought on part and part,             105
       Till the Prince came, who parted either part.
LADY MONTAGUE  O where is Romeo? saw you him today?
       Right glad I am he was not at this fray.
BENVOLIO  Madam, an hour before the worshipped sun
       Peered forth the golden window of the east,                   110
       A troubled mind drive me to walk abroad,
       Where underneath the grove of sycamore,
       That westward rooteth from this city side,
       So early walking did I see your son;
       Towards him I made, but he was ware of me,                    115
       And stole into the covert of the wood;
       I, measuring his affections by my own,
       Which then most sought where most might not be found,
       Being one too many by my weary self,
       Pursued my humour, not pursuing his,                          120
       And gladly shunned who gladly fled from me.
MONTAGUE  Many a morning hath he there been seen,
       With tears augmenting the fresh morning's dew,
       Adding to clouds more clouds with his deep sighs,
       But all so soon as the all-cheering sun                       125
       Should in the farthest east begin to draw
       The shady curtains from Aurora's bed,
       Away from light steals home my heavy son,
       And private in his chamber pens himself,
       Shuts up his windows, locks fair daylight out,                130
       And makes himself an artificial night:
       Black and portentous must this humour prove,
       Unless good counsel may the cause remove.

Romeo and Juliet

*Benvolio promises to find out the cause of Romeo's sadness. Romeo says it is because his love for Rosaline (whom he doesn't name) is not returned. He suddenly notices the signs of the riot.*

## 1 Parents question children (in groups of four or five)

Montague says that he and his friends have questioned Romeo about why he keeps so much to himself, but without success. Romeo just won't tell.

Improvise this questioning of Romeo by his father and other adults who wish to find out the cause of his sadness. After the improvisation, each group member reads Montague's speech (lines 137–46) to the group to see if it comes over as exasperation or puzzlement, or as some other mood.

## 2 Two lines to exercise your imagination

'the bud bit with an envious worm'
'Love, whose view is muffled still'

Either prepare a tableau (a still photograph) of each of these lines or make a drawing up to illustrate each. It may help you to know that the second line probably refers to blindfolded Cupid (see page 50).

## 3 What's the play all about? (in groups of three to six)

Here's what one student said of line 166:

'This line ("Here's much to do with hate, but more with love") is really what the play is all about. It's the most important line of all.'

Talk together, from what you know of the play so far, about whether you agree with her view.

---

**shrift** confession
**proof** experience
**muffled** blindfold

BENVOLIO My noble uncle, do you know the cause?
MONTAGUE I neither know it, nor can learn of him.                                    135
BENVOLIO Have you importuned him by any means?
MONTAGUE Both by myself and many other friends,
　　　　But he, his own affections' counsellor,
　　　　Is to himself (I will not say how true)
　　　　But to himself so secret and so close,                                        140
　　　　So far from sounding and discovery,
　　　　As is the bud bit with an envious worm
　　　　Ere he can spread his sweet leaves to the air,
　　　　Or dedicate his beauty to the sun.
　　　　Could we but learn from whence his sorrows grow,                     145
　　　　We would as willingly give cure as know.

　　　　　　　　　*Enter* ROMEO.

BENVOLIO See where he comes. So please you step aside,
　　　　I'll know his grievance or be much denied.
MONTAGUE I would thou wert so happy by thy stay
　　　　To hear true shrift. Come, madam, let's away.                           150
　　　　　　　　　*Exeunt [Montague and Lady Montague]*
BENVOLIO Good morrow, cousin.
ROMEO　　　　　　　　　　Is the day so young?
BENVOLIO But new struck nine.
ROMEO　　　　　　　　　　Ay me, sad hours seem long.
　　　　Was that my father that went hence so fast?
BENVOLIO It was. What sadness lengthens Romeo's hours?
ROMEO Not having that, which, having, makes them short.              155
BENVOLIO In love?
ROMEO Out –
BENVOLIO Of love?
ROMEO Out of her favour where I am in love.
BENVOLIO Alas that Love, so gentle in his view,                                   160
　　　　Should be so tyrannous and rough in proof!
ROMEO Alas that Love, whose view is muffled still,
　　　　Should, without eyes, see pathways to his will!
　　　　Where shall we dine? O me! what fray was here?
　　　　Yet tell me not, for I have heard it all:                                       165
　　　　Here's much to do with hate, but more with love:
　　　　Why then, O brawling love, O loving hate,
　　　　O any thing of nothing first create!

13

*Romeo, melancholy because he loves a girl (Rosaline) who does not love him, plays with words on how love confuses and mixes up, turning order into chaos.*

## 1 Romeo's language (in pairs)

Take a closer look at Romeo's language. Here's a different way of setting out parts of lines 167–72

loving *v* hate
heavy *v* lightness
serious *v* vanity
misshapen chaos *v* well-seeming forms
feather *v* lead
bright *v* smoke
cold *v* fire
sick *v* health
still-waking *v* sleep

It was fashionable in the love poetry of Shakespeare's time to put together such contradictory words. These strange oppositions (e.g. 'loving hate') are called **oxymorons** (see page 212).

With your partner, choose one pair of words from the list above and prepare three tableaux. These three frozen pictures show the two separate words (e.g. 'loving' and 'hate'), then show the oxymoron ('loving hate'). The class guesses which oxymoron each pair has chosen.

Also try making up oxymorons of your own for the class to guess. If you want a few 'starters', fill in the blanks:

slow _____
cowardly _____

**coz** cousin
**fume** breath
**gall** bitter poison
**sadness** seriousness (line 190).
  Notice Romeo's word-play in
  line 193
**mark-man** marksman: an archer
  who hits the target (mark)
**Dian** Diana, goddess of hunting,
  and chastity. She avoided Cupid's
  arrows
**proof** armour

14

O heavy lightness, serious vanity,
Misshapen chaos of well-seeming forms, 170
Feather of lead, bright smoke, cold fire, sick health,
Still-waking sleep, that is not what it is!
This love feel I, that feel no love in this.
Dost thou not laugh?
BENVOLIO                         No, coz, I rather weep.
ROMEO Good heart, at what?
BENVOLIO                         At thy good heart's oppression. 175
ROMEO Why, such is love's transgression:
Griefs of mine own lie heavy in my breast,
Which thou wilt propagate to have it pressed
With more of thine; this love that thou hast shown
Doth add more grief to too much of mine own. 180
Love is a smoke made with the fume of sighs,
Being purged, a fire sparkling in lovers' eyes,
Being vexed, a sea nourished with loving tears.
What is it else? a madness most discreet,
A choking gall, and a preserving sweet. 185
Farewell, my coz.
BENVOLIO             Soft, I will go along;
And if you leave me so, you do me wrong.
ROMEO Tut, I have lost myself, I am not here,
This is not Romeo, he's some other where.
BENVOLIO Tell me in sadness, who is that you love? 190
ROMEO What, shall I groan and tell thee?
BENVOLIO                         Groan? why, no;
But sadly tell me, who?
ROMEO Bid a sick man in sadness make his will –
A word ill urged to one that is so ill:
In sadness, cousin, I do love a woman. 195
BENVOLIO I aimed so near, when I supposed you loved.
ROMEO A right good mark-man! and she's fair I love.
BENVOLIO A right fair mark, fair coz, is soonest hit.
ROMEO Well, in that hit you miss: she'll not be hit
With Cupid's arrow, she hath Dian's wit; 200
And in strong proof of chastity well armed,
From Love's weak childish bow she lives uncharmed.

*Romeo complains that because she refuses to marry, the woman he loves will leave no children. Her beauty dies with her. Benvolio advises him to look at other girls – that will cure him! Romeo isn't convinced.*

## 1 But is Romeo really in love? (in small groups)

Today, many people think that because Romeo uses this elaborate way of speaking, his emotions are 'artificial', not coming from the heart. But what do you think? Does this manner of speaking show that he is really in love, as he claims to be, or just infatuated? Speak Romeo's language and talk about whether it strikes you as really sincere and heartfelt.

Nicholas Hilliard's painting of an Elizabethan courtier echoes the melancholy mood of Romeo: leaning languorously on a tree, hand on heart, and caught by rosebush thorns, the symbol of unrequited passion.

**stay the siege** submit to the assault (notice Romeo's military metaphor)

**forsworn to love** taken an oath not to fall in love
**pay that doctrine** teach that lesson

She will not stay the siege of loving terms,
Nor bide th'encounter of assailing eyes,
Nor ope her lap to saint-seducing gold.                    205
O, she is rich in beauty, only poor
That when she dies, with beauty dies her store.
BENVOLIO Then she hath sworn that she will still live chaste?
ROMEO She hath, and in that sparing makes huge waste;
For beauty starved with her severity                       210
Cuts beauty off from all posterity.
She is too fair, too wise, wisely too fair,
To merit bliss by making me despair.
She hath forsworn to love, and in that vow
Do I live dead, that live to tell it now.                  215
BENVOLIO Be ruled by me, forget to think of her.
ROMEO O teach me how I should forget to think.
BENVOLIO By giving liberty unto thine eyes,
Examine other beauties.
ROMEO                           'Tis the way
To call hers (exquisite) in question more:                 220
These happy masks that kiss fair ladies' brows,
Being black, puts us in mind they hide the fair;
He that is strucken blind cannot forget
The precious treasure of his eyesight lost;
Show me a mistress that is passing fair,                   225
What doth her beauty serve but as a note
Where I may read who passed that passing fair?
Farewell, thou canst not teach me to forget.
BENVOLIO I'll pay that doctrine, or else die in debt.

                                                    *Exeunt*

*Paris wishes to marry Juliet. Capulet says his daughter is still only thirteen, but he will agree if Juliet consents. He invites Paris to a party that night.*

## 1 What were Capulet and Paris talking about? (in pairs)

Capulet and Paris enter in the middle of a conversation. Improvise some of the things they have been saying together before they entered. Remember, Capulet has already been involved in the action of Scene 1; Paris has not been involved. Try to make your improvised conversation lead up naturally to the opening line: 'But Montague is bound as well as I'.

## 2 Have all Capulet's other children died?

Make a drawing to illustrate line 14:

'Earth hath swallowed all my hopes but she'.

## 3 Lines 32–3 – can you work them out?

Most people find these two lines very difficult, so don't worry if you have problems with them. They echo Benvolio's advice to Romeo in Scene 1 ('Examine other beauties' – look at other girls). The general sense seems to be: 'When you see the other girls at my party, my daughter might or might not be the one you'll like most'. If you were directing the play, and the actor playing Capulet asked you how to make the meaning as clear as possible to Paris and the audience, what would you suggest?

---

**Clown** (servant) in most modern productions this is usually Peter, the Nurse's servant
**suit** request to marry
**marred** spoilt

**well-apparelled** well-dressed
**fennel buds** fennel (a herb) was thought to provoke passion. Here it implies 'young women'

# ACT 1   SCENE 2

*Enter* CAPULET, COUNTY PARIS, *and the* CLOWN [SERVANT *to* CAPULET].

CAPULET  But Montague is bound as well as I,
    In penalty alike, and 'tis not hard, I think,
    For men so old as we to keep the peace.
PARIS  Of honourable reckoning are you both,
    And pity 'tis, you lived at odds so long. 5
    But now, my lord, what say you to my suit?
CAPULET  But saying o'er what I have said before:
    My child is yet a stranger in the world,
    She hath not seen the change of fourteen years;
    Let two more summers wither in their pride, 10
    Ere we may think her ripe to be a bride.
PARIS  Younger than she are happy mothers made.
CAPULET  And too soon marred are those so early made.
    Earth hath swallowed all my hopes but she;
    She's the hopeful lady of my earth. 15
    But woo her, gentle Paris, get her heart,
    My will to her consent is but a part;
    And she agreed, within her scope of choice
    Lies my consent and fair according voice.
    This night I hold an old accustomed feast, 20
    Whereto I have invited many a guest,
    Such as I love, and you among the store,
    One more, most welcome, makes my number more.
    At my poor house look to behold this night
    Earth-treading stars that make dark heaven light. 25
    Such comfort as do lusty young men feel
    When well-apparelled April on the heel
    Of limping winter treads, even such delight
    Among fresh fennel buds shall you this night
    Inherit at my house; hear all, all see; 30
    And like her most whose merit most shall be;
    Which on more view of many, mine, being one,
    May stand in number, though in reck'ning none.

*Capulet orders his servant to deliver party invitations. The servant can't read, so he asks Romeo to read the names.*

---

## 1 Is the servant clever or stupid? (in pairs)

The servant, who cannot read, is given a list of names. As he talks (lines 39–40), he muddles up workers and their tools (a shoemaker uses a last, a tailor a yard, etc.). Imagine you are directing the play. The actor playing the servant asks whether he should play him as dull-witted or clever. Is the servant in fact cleverer than he seems? What do you say, and why?

To help you, read lines 38–43 with your partner: first, as if the servant is stupid, then as if he is quick-witted.

## 2 Benvolio's advice (in groups of four)

Benvolio's advice to Romeo (lines 44–9) is that the cure for love is to look at other girls. Here, he says the same thing in five different ways. Work out how you can show, without words, each part of the advice. A hint: it's probably easiest to begin with 'pain' (line 45), then 'giddy', then 'grief', then 'infection'. Finally, see if you can make up a mime for 'fire'.

Show your five actions to the class.

Shakespeare kept returning to the image of fire used to fight fire. By the time he wrote *Coriolanus* in 1608, he had reduced it all to a single line 'one fire drives out one fire; one nail, one nail'.

---

**yard** a tailor's measuring rod
**last** a shoemaker's device to hold a shoe
**holp** helped

**plantain leaf** a leaf used to heal cuts and grazes
**god-den** good evening
**rest you merry** farewell

Come go with me. [*To Servant*] Go, sirrah, trudge about
Through fair Verona, find those persons out                                    35
Whose names are written there [*Gives a paper.*], and to
   them say,
My house and welcome on their pleasure stay.
                                                      *Exit* [*with Paris*]
SERVANT Find them out whose names are written here! It is written
   that the shoemaker should meddle with his yard and the tailor with
   his last, the fisher with his pencil and the painter with his nets;     40
   but I am sent to find those persons whose names are here writ, and
   can never find what names the writing person hath here writ. I must
   to the learnèd. In good time!

                  *Enter* BENVOLIO *and* ROMEO.

BENVOLIO Tut, man, one fire burns out another's burning,
           One pain is lessened by another's anguish;                        45
           Turn giddy, and be holp by backward turning;
           One desperate grief cures with another's languish:
           Take thou some new infection to thy eye,
           And the rank poison of the old will die.
ROMEO Your plantain leaf is excellent for that.                              50
BENVOLIO For what, I pray thee?
ROMEO                              For your broken shin.
BENVOLIO Why, Romeo, art thou mad?
ROMEO Not mad, but bound more than a madman is:
           Shut up in prison, kept without my food,
           Whipt and tormented, and – God-den, good fellow.                  55
SERVANT God gi' god-den. I pray, sir, can you read?
ROMEO Ay, mine own fortune in my misery.
SERVANT Perhaps you have learned it without book; but I pray, can
   you read any thing you see?
ROMEO Ay, if I know the letters and the language.                            60
SERVANT Ye say honestly, rest you merry.
ROMEO Stay, fellow, I can read.
                        *He reads the letter.*
           'Signior Martino and his wife and daughters,
           County Anselme and his beauteous sisters,
           The lady widow of Vitruvio,                                       65
           Signior Placentio and his lovely nieces,
           Mercutio and his brother Valentine,

*Romeo discovers that Rosaline has been invited to Capulet's party. Benvolio urges Romeo to go. There he will see women more beautiful than Rosaline.*

---

## 1 The invitation list (in groups of ten or more)

The names on the list of guests (lines 63–71) roll off the tongue. One person acts as Master (or Mistress) of Ceremonies. He or she will announce the guests, line by line. Everyone else chooses a part and decides how to enter. Choose your part (or parts) and prepare your grand entrance to Capulet's party. At least twenty-three persons are named, so double parts and make two entrances!

## 2 How does Romeo react? (in pairs)

Romeo, reading the list, suddenly discovers (line 69) that Rosaline, the woman he thinks he loves, is coming to the party. How does he react at that moment? Read the list to your partner and react to the name 'Rosaline' as you think Romeo would react.

## 3 'Turn tears to fires' (line 89)

Romeo continues to protest that his love for Rosaline will never change. He even says (lines 88–91) that if he did see someone more beautiful than Rosaline, his eyes would burn out because they were liars, unfaithful to the true belief: Rosaline's beauty. Romeo's lines seem to be inspired by the practice of burning heretics at the stake.

'Transparent heretics, be burnt for liars.'

---

**unattainted** unbiased
**transparent heretics** obvious
  disbelievers
**scant** scarcely

                    Mine uncle Capulet, his wife and daughters,
                    My fair niece Rosaline, and Livia,
                    Signior Valentio and his cousin Tybalt,                    70
                    Lucio and the lively Helena.'
              A fair assembly: whither should they come?
SERVANT Up.
ROMEO Whither? to supper?
SERVANT To our house.                                                         75
ROMEO Whose house?
SERVANT My master's.
ROMEO Indeed I should have asked thee that before.
SERVANT Now I'll tell you without asking. My master is the great rich
     Capulet, and if you be not of the house of Montagues, I pray come        80
     and crush a cup of wine. Rest you merry.                    [*Exit*]
BENVOLIO At this same ancient feast of Capulet's
              Sups the fair Rosaline whom thou so loves,
              With all the admirèd beauties of Verona:
              Go thither, and with unattainted eye                            85
              Compare her face with some that I shall show,
              And I will make thee think thy swan a crow.
ROMEO When the devout religion of mine eye
              Maintains such falsehood, then turn tears to fires;
              And these who, often drowned, could never die,                  90
              Transparent heretics, be burnt for liars.
              One fairer than my love! the all-seeing sun
              Ne'er saw her match since first the world begun.
BENVOLIO Tut, you saw her fair, none else being by,
              Herself poised with herself in either eye;                      95
              But in that crystal scales let there be weighed
              Your lady's love against some other maid
              That I will show you shining at this feast,
              And she shall scant show well that now seems best.
ROMEO I'll go along no such sight to be shown,                                100
              But to rejoice in splendour of mine own.
                                                          [*Exeunt*]

*Lady Capulet and the Nurse discuss Juliet's age.*

---

## 1 The Nurse – what's she like? (groups of three or four)

Read aloud all the Nurse says from line 2 to line 63. Each person reads only a little of the Nurse's language (not more than two lines, sometimes only one or two words), then hands the speech on to the next group member. Just read a short piece that makes sense on its own, then hand on. Read the lines two or three times in this way, speaking your own short extracts as you think the Nurse would say them.

Afterwards, talk about the Nurse, about what kind of person you think she is. Make a list of the words your group would use to describe her. Compare the views the class has of the Nurse's character.

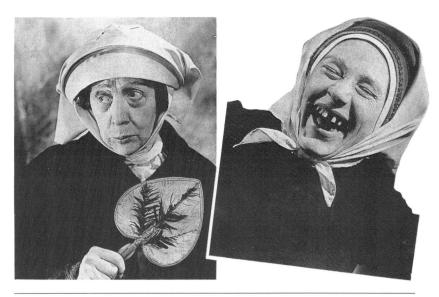

---

**teen** sorrow
**Lammas-tide** 1 August (Lady
  Mass). Juliet will be fourteen on
  Lammas-eve (31 July)

**laid wormwood to my**
  **dug** rubbed bitter-tasting plant on
  her nipple (to wean Juliet)

## ACT 1    SCENE 3
## A room in Capulet's mansion

*Enter* CAPULET'S WIFE *and* NURSE.

LADY CAPULET  Nurse, where's my daughter? call her forth to me.
NURSE  Now by my maidenhead at twelve year old,
    I bade her come. What, lamb! What, ladybird!
    God forbid, where's this girl? What, Juliet!

*Enter* JULIET.

JULIET  How now, who calls?                          5
NURSE  Your mother.
JULIET  Madam, I am here, what is your will?
LADY CAPULET  This is the matter. Nurse, give leave a while,
    We must talk in secret. Nurse, come back again,
    I have remembered me, thou s' hear our counsel.    10
    Thou knowest my daughter's of a pretty age.
NURSE  Faith, I can tell her age unto an hour.
LADY CAPULET  She's not fourteen.
NURSE                    I'll lay fourteen of my teeth –
    And yet to my teen be it spoken, I have but four –
    She's not fourteen. How long is it now           15
    To Lammas-tide?
LADY CAPULET           A fortnight and odd days.
NURSE  Even or odd, of all days in the year,
    Come Lammas-eve at night shall she be fourteen.
    Susan and she – God rest all Christian souls! –
    Were of an age. Well, Susan is with God,          20
    She was too good for me. But as I said,
    On Lammas-eve at night shall she be fourteen,
    That shall she, marry, I remember it well.
    'Tis since the earthquake now aleven years,
    And she was weaned – I never shall forget it –    25
    Of all the days of the year, upon that day;
    For I had then laid wormwood to my dug,
    Sitting in the sun under the dove-house wall.
    My lord and you were then at Mantua –
    Nay, I do bear a brain – but as I said,          30

*The Nurse reminisces about Juliet's childhood. Lady Capulet begins to talk to Juliet about marriage.*

---

## 1 What does Lady Capulet think about the Nurse?
(in groups of four or five)

Improvise a scene later that day between Lady Capulet, her husband and his guests when she tells him what the Nurse has said. Remember Lady Capulet has very high status in Verona. What does she reply when her husband and his friends keep pressing her for details about the Nurse's story?

## 2 Direct the scene (in pairs)

Work out stage directions for this scene so far. Advise Juliet and Lady Capulet on how they should behave during the Nurse's long story (lines 17–63). Pick out any of the Nurse's lines or words that you think are particularly important because Juliet or Lady Capulet would respond in some obvious way to them. Suggest how the actors might react to these words.

---

**shake!** look lively! (shake a leg!)
**I trow** I'm sure
**th'rood** Christ's cross

**holidam** 'holiness', or Virgin Mary (holy dame)
**stinted** stopped (crying)
**cock'rel's stone** cockerel's testicle

When it did taste the wormwood on the nipple
Of my dug, and felt it bitter, pretty fool,
To see it tetchy and fall out wi'th'dug!
'Shake!' quoth the dove-house; 'twas no need, I trow,
To bid me trudge.                                        35
And since that time it is aleven years,
For then she could stand high-lone; nay, by th'rood,
She could have run and waddled all about;
For even the day before, she broke her brow,
And then my husband – God be with his soul,              40
'A was a merry man – took up the child.
'Yea', quoth he, 'dost thou fall upon thy face?
Thou wilt fall backward when thou hast more wit,
Wilt thou not, Jule?' And by my holidam,
The pretty wretch left crying, and said 'Ay'.            45
To see now how a jest shall come about!
I warrant, and I should live a thousand years,
I never should forget it: 'Wilt thou not, Jule?' quoth he,
And, pretty fool, it stinted, and said 'Ay'.
LADY CAPULET Enough of this, I pray thee hold thy peace.   50
NURSE Yes, madam, yet I cannot choose but laugh,
To think it should leave crying, and say 'Ay':
And yet I warrant it had upon it brow
A bump as big as a young cock'rel's stone,
A perilous knock, and it cried bitterly.                 55
'Yea', quoth my husband, 'fall'st upon thy face?
Thou wilt fall backward when thou comest to age,
Wilt thou not, Jule?' It stinted, and said 'Ay'.
JULIET And stint thou too, I pray thee, Nurse, say I.
NURSE Peace, I have done. God mark thee to his grace,      60
Thou wast the prettiest babe that e'er I nursed.
And I might live to see thee married once,
I have my wish.
LADY CAPULET Marry, that 'marry' is the very theme
I came to talk of. Tell me, daughter Juliet,             65
How stands your dispositions to be married?
JULIET It is an honour that I dream not of.
NURSE An honour! were not I thine only nurse,
I would say thou hadst sucked wisdom from thy teat.

---

*Lady Capulet gives her reasons why Juliet should think of marriage. She tells her daughter of Paris' love, praising him in elaborate style. A servant tells them the party guests have arrived.*

### 1 Juliet – first impressions (in pairs)

Juliet says little throughout this scene. Read all her lines, then talk together about your impressions of her so far.

### 2 'Man of wax' (in groups of four)

No one is really quite sure what line 77 means. It could be that the Nurse says Paris is a perfect man, like a sculptor's model in wax. Or perhaps she means something else. Talk together about possible meanings. What might 'man of wax' mean if you used it to describe someone living today?

### 3 Paris – described in a sonnet (in pairs)

Lady Capulet's lines 82–95 read like a sonnet. Sit facing each other and read the lines aloud, each person reading just one line at a time. As you read your line, try to perform an action with the book you have in your hand (the whole sonnet is an elaborate comparison of Paris with a book). Some lines you'll find quite easy to accompany with an action. Others are more difficult, especially lines 90–91, 'The fish lives in the sea . . . the fair within to hide'. This seems to mean that just as fishes are at home in the sea, so good books deserve good covers, and handsome men deserve beautiful wives. But no one can be absolutely sure what it means.

**married lineament** harmonious feature
**margent** margin
**endart** pierce like a dart
**the County stays** Count Paris is waiting

28

LADY CAPULET  Well, think of marriage now; younger than you,                70
    Here in Verona, ladies of esteem,
    Are made already mothers. By my count,
    I was your mother much upon these years
    That you are now a maid. Thus then in brief:
    The valiant Paris seeks you for his love.                75
NURSE  A man, young lady! lady, such a man
    As all the world – Why, he's a man of wax.
LADY CAPULET  Verona's summer hath not such a flower.
NURSE  Nay, he's a flower, in faith, a very flower.
LADY CAPULET  What say you, can you love the gentleman?                80
    This night you shall behold him at our feast;
    Read o'er the volume of young Paris' face,
    And find delight writ there with beauty's pen;
    Examine every married lineament,
    And see how one another lends content;                85
    And what obscured in this fair volume lies
    Find written in the margent of his eyes.
    This precious book of love, this unbound lover,
    To beautify him, only lacks a cover.
    The fish lives in the sea, and 'tis much pride                90
    For fair without the fair within to hide;
    That book in many's eyes doth share the glory
    That in gold clasps locks in the golden story:
    So shall you share all that he doth possess,
    By having him, making yourself no less.                95
NURSE  No less! nay, bigger women grow by men.
LADY CAPULET  Speak briefly, can you like of Paris' love?
JULIET  I'll look to like, if looking liking move;
    But no more deep will I endart mine eye
    Than your consent gives strength to make it fly.                100

*Enter* SERVINGMAN.

SERVINGMAN  Madam, the guests are come, supper served up, you
    called, my young lady asked for, the Nurse cursed in the pantry,
    and every thing in extremity. I must hence to wait, I beseech you
    follow straight.                                                                    [*Exit*]
LADY CAPULET  We follow thee. Juliet, the County stays.                105
NURSE  Go, girl, seek happy nights to happy days.

                                   *Exeunt*

*Romeo and his friends, carrying masks and torches, prepare for their visit to Capulet's party. Mercutio tries to laugh Romeo out of his sadness.*

## 1 Gatecrashing (in groups of four or five)

Romeo and his friends are about to gatecrash Capulet's party. It was the custom of such uninvited guests to have a speech prepared and to perform a dance for the guests. Benvolio argues that such speeches are old-fashioned and long-winded ('The date is out of such prolixity') and that they should just perform their dance and leave ('We'll measure them a measure and be gone').

Imagine you are a group about to visit a party you've not been invited to. Discuss what you'll do to make yourselves acceptable. Then show your idea, in action, to the class.

## 2 Prompting (in pairs)

Benvolio's two lines 7 and 8 seem to be Shakespeare having a joke about actors not remembering their lines and having to be prompted. Talk together about whether you think Shakespeare was having a dig at the actor who speaks the Prologue.

## 3 Language – something to think about

Elizabethans were amused and fascinated by language, especially by **puns**. Puns are words which sound the same but have different meanings. In the lines opposite you'll find many, e.g. measure/ measure, soles/soul, soar/sore, bound/bound, pricks/prick, visor/ visor. There's a great deal of punning throughout *Romeo and Juliet*. Look out for other examples – and see page 213.

**Tartar's painted bow of lath** an oriental bow (shaped like an upper lip). Here, made of thin wood and held by Cupid (see picture on page 50)
**crow-keeper** scarecrow

**measure** dance (notice Benvolio's puns)
**case** mask
**A visor for a visor** a mask for an ugly face
**cote** notice

# ACT 1   SCENE 4
## A street outside Capulet's mansion

Enter ROMEO, MERCUTIO, BENVOLIO, with five or six other MASKERS,
TORCH-BEARERS.

ROMEO  What, shall this speech be spoke for our excuse?
Or shall we on without apology?
BENVOLIO  The date is out of such prolixity:
We'll have no Cupid hoodwinked with a scarf,
Bearing a Tartar's painted bow of lath,                               5
Scaring the ladies like a crow-keeper,
Nor no without-book prologue, faintly spoke
After the prompter, for our entrance;
But let them measure us by what they will,
We'll measure them a measure and be gone.                             10
ROMEO  Give me a torch, I am not for this ambling;
Being but heavy, I will bear the light.
MERCUTIO  Nay, gentle Romeo, we must have you dance.
ROMEO  Not I, believe me. You have dancing shoes
With nimble soles, I have a soul of lead                              15
So stakes me to the ground I cannot move.
MERCUTIO  You are a lover, borrow Cupid's wings,
And soar with them above a common bound.
ROMEO  I am too sore enpiercèd with his shaft
To soar with his light feathers, and so bound                        20
I cannot bound a pitch above dull woe:
Under love's heavy burden do I sink.
MERCUTIO  And to sink in it should you burden love,
Too great oppression for a tender thing.
ROMEO  Is love a tender thing? it is too rough,                       25
Too rude, too boist'rous, and it pricks like thorn.
MERCUTIO  If love be rough with you, be rough with love:
Prick love for pricking, and you beat love down.
Give me a case to put my visage in, [*Puts on a mask.*]
A visor for a visor! what care I                                     30
What curious eye doth cote deformities?
Here are the beetle brows shall blush for me.

*Romeo refuses to be cheered up, in spite of Mercutio's joking. He has no wish to join in the dance. Mercutio begins to tell of Queen Mab.*

An artist's vision of Queen Mab. How does it compare with Mercutio's description?

**senseless rushes** green rushes used to cover floors – can you think why Romeo calls them 'senseless'?
**grandsire phrase** old saying
**dun** mouse-coloured

**Dun** horse or 'stick in the mud'. An Elizabethan Christmas game was 'Dun-in-the-mire': partygoers pulled a log out of an imaginary marsh
**burn daylight** waste time

BENVOLIO Come knock and enter, and no sooner in,
    But every man betake him to his legs.
ROMEO A torch for me: let wantons light of heart     35
    Tickle the senseless rushes with their heels;
    For I am proverbed with a grandsire phrase,
    I'll be a candle-holder and look on:
    The game was ne'er so fair, and I am done.
MERCUTIO Tut, dun's the mouse, the constable's own word.    40
    If thou art Dun, we'll draw thee from the mire,
    Or (save your reverence) love, wherein thou stickest
    Up to the ears. Come, we burn daylight, ho!
ROMEO Nay, that's not so.
MERCUTIO              I mean, sir, in delay
    We waste our lights in vain, like lights by day.    45
    Take our good meaning, for our judgement sits
    Five times in that ere once in our five wits.
ROMEO And we mean well in going to this mask,
    But 'tis no wit to go.
MERCUTIO              Why, may one ask?
ROMEO I dreamt a dream tonight.
MERCUTIO               And so did I.    50
ROMEO Well, what was yours?
MERCUTIO               That dreamers often lie.
ROMEO In bed asleep, while they do dream things true.
MERCUTIO O then I see Queen Mab hath been with you:
    She is the fairies' midwife, and she comes
    In shape no bigger than an agate-stone    55
    On the forefinger of an alderman,
    Drawn with a team of little atomi
    Over men's noses as they lie asleep.
    Her chariot is an empty hazel-nut,
    Made by the joiner squirrel or old grub,    60
    Time out a'mind the fairies' coachmakers:
    Her waggon-spokes made of long spinners' legs,
    The cover of the wings of grasshoppers,
    Her traces of the smallest spider web,
    Her collars of the moonshine's wat'ry beams,    65
    Her whip of cricket's bone, the lash of film,
    Her waggoner a small grey-coated gnat,
    Not half so big as a round little worm

*Mercutio continues his description of Queen Mab. He dismisses dreams as nothing but idle fantasies.*

---

### 1 What does Queen Mab do to people? (in pairs)

In lines 70–94, Mercutio describes what Queen Mab does to different people. One person reads the speech a line at a time, the other mimes the actions described. Then change over reader and mimer.

Talk together about which actions you think best fit each line. Show your final version to the class. Don't be afraid to use your imagination – that's what Mercutio is doing!

### 2 Queen Mab today – your version (in pairs or small groups)

Take lines 59–94 and write your own version of Queen Mab for today. There are two sections to the speech:

- the description of her carriage (lines 59–69)
- what she does to people (lines 70–94).

Use Shakespeare's language as the basis of your own Queen Mab. You might wish to substitute one word at a time, or line for line. Or you may prefer to write in your own style. As the group works together you'll find you produce a rich fund of ideas.

Put actions to your version and show it to the other groups.

---

**cur'sies** curtsies, bowing and scraping
**smelling out a suit** gaining money by helping someone at court
**tithe-pig** pigs were sometimes given to clergyman as tithes (a tenth part of one's income)

**benefice** source of income, a paid position
**Spanish blades** high-quality swords or fashionable young men
**healths** drinks (or toasts, as in 'cheers')
**elf-locks** tangled, knotted hair

```
              Pricked from the lazy finger of a maid.
              And in this state she gallops night by night          70
              Through lovers' brains, and then they dream of love,
              O'er courtiers' knees, that dream on cur'sies straight,
              O'er lawyers' fingers, who straight dream on fees,
              O'er ladies' lips, who straight on kisses dream,
              Which oft the angry Mab with blisters plagues,         75
              Because their breaths with sweetmeats tainted are.
              Sometime she gallops o'er a courtier's nose,
              And then dreams he of smelling out a suit;
              And sometime comes she with a tithe-pig's tail
              Tickling a parson's nose as 'a lies asleep,            80
              Then he dreams of another benefice.
              Sometime she driveth o'er a soldier's neck,
              And then dreams he of cutting foreign throats,
              Of breaches, ambuscadoes, Spanish blades,
              Of healths five fathom deep; and then anon             85
              Drums in his ear, at which he starts and wakes,
              And being thus frighted, swears a prayer or two,
              And sleeps again. This is that very Mab
              That plats the manes of horses in the night,
              And bakes the elf-locks in foul sluttish hairs,        90
              Which, once untangled, much misfortune bodes.
              This is the hag, when maids lie on their backs,
              That presses them and learns them first to bear,
              Making them women of good carriage.
              This is she –
ROMEO                     Peace, peace, Mercutio, peace!             95
              Thou talk'st of nothing.
MERCUTIO                       True, I talk of dreams,
              Which are the children of an idle brain,
              Begot of nothing but vain fantasy,
              Which is as thin of substance as the air,
              And more inconstant than the wind, who woos           100
              Even now the frozen bosom of the north,
              And being angered puffs away from thence,
              Turning his side to the dew-dropping south.
BENVOLIO This wind you talk of blows us from ourselves:
              Supper is done, and we shall come too late.            105
```

*In spite of his fearful misgivings, Romeo decides to go along with the others to Capulet's party. The following scene begins with Capulet's servants joking together as they prepare for the dancing.*

## 1 What was Romeo's fearful dream? (in pairs)

Romeo looks uneasily into the future and has a premonition of death. His tone is ominous, filled with foreboding. He uses legal language prophesying that his premature ('untimely') death will result from what he begins tonight ('date') by going to Capulet's feast. His life will be the penalty ('forfeit') he must pay when the time is up ('expire the term').

Earlier (line 50), Romeo spoke of his dream. Talk together about lines 106–11 and work out what you think Romeo's dream might have been. You may find it helpful to pick out all the words in these six lines that describe fear or loss. No one really knows what Romeo dreamed, so don't be afraid to use your imagination.

## 2 Act out the servants' lines 1–14 (in groups of four)

You'll find you can perform this tiny bustling scene-opening (only fourteen lines) in all kinds of ways. In groups of four, act out the lines, inventing as much 'business' as you like to suit the words.

---

**He that hath the steerage of my course** God, who guides my life
**servingmen** in modern productions often played by Peter, Sampson and Gregory
**trencher** wooden dish
**join-stools** wooden stools
**look to the plate** clear away the silverware
**marchpane** marzipan

ROMEO I fear too early, for my mind misgives
        Some consequence yet hanging in the stars
        Shall bitterly begin his fearful date
        With this night's revels, and expire the term
        Of a despisèd life closed in my breast,        110
        By some vile forfeit of untimely death.
        But He that hath the steerage of my course
        Direct my sail! On, lusty gentlemen.
BENVOLIO Strike, drum.
      *They march about the stage [and stand to one side].*

## ACT 1   SCENE 5
## The Great Hall in Capulet's mansion

      SERVINGMEN come forth with napkins.

FIRST SERVINGMAN Where's Potpan, that he helps not to take away?
  He shift a trencher? he scrape a trencher?
SECOND SERVINGMAN When good manners shall lie all in one or two
  men's hands, and they unwashed too, 'tis a foul thing.
FIRST SERVINGMAN Away with the join-stools, remove the court-   5
  cupboard, look to the plate. Good thou, save me a piece of
  marchpane, and as thou loves me, let the porter let in Susan
  Grindstone and Nell.
           *[Exit Second Servingman]*
  Anthony and Potpan!

      *[Enter two more SERVINGMEN.]*

THIRD SERVINGMAN Ay, boy, ready.         10
FIRST SERVINGMAN You are looked for and called for, asked for and
  sought for, in the great chamber.
FOURTH SERVINGMAN We cannot be here and there too. Cheerly,
  boys, be brisk a while, and the longer liver take all.
           *[They retire behind]*

*Capulet welcomes the dancers. He reminisces with his cousin about past times. Romeo catches sight of Juliet for the first time.*

Maskers and dancers, Royal Shakespeare Company, 1976.

## 1 The dance (in groups of eight)

Work out a dance sequence for the two stage directions: 'Music plays' and 'And they dance'.

You can work out any dance you like – but all members of the group should be involved together. There may not be time to work on this in lesson time. Practise at break or lunch-time, and present your dance sequence at the start of a later lesson.

**Maskers** masked dancers
**walk a bout** dance
**visor** mask
**Berlady** by our Lady (the Virgin Mary)

**Pentecost** Whit Sunday, fifty days after Easter
**ward** under twenty-one (and so having a guardian)

*Enter* [CAPULET, LADY CAPULET, JULIET, TYBALT *and his* PAGE, NURSE, *and*] *all the* GUESTS *and* GENTLEWOMEN *to the Maskers.*

CAPULET  Welcome, gentlemen! Ladies that have their toes                15
     Unplagued with corns will walk a bout with you.
     Ah, my mistresses, which of you all
     Will now deny to dance? She that makes dainty,
     She I'll swear hath corns. Am I come near ye now?
     Welcome, gentlemen! I have seen the day                20
     That I have worn a visor and could tell
     A whispering tale in a fair lady's ear,
     Such as would please; 'tis gone, 'tis gone, 'tis gone.
     You are welcome, gentlemen. Come, musicians, play.
                  *Music plays.*
     A hall, a hall, give room! and foot it, girls.
                *And they dance.*                25
     More light, you knaves, and turn the tables up;
     And quench the fire, the room is grown too hot.
     Ah, sirrah, this unlooked-for sport comes well.
     Nay, sit, nay, sit, good Cousin Capulet,
     For you and I are past our dancing days.                30
     How long is't now since last yourself and I
     Were in a mask?
COUSIN CAPULET         Berlady, thirty years.
CAPULET  What, man, 'tis not so much, 'tis not so much:
     'Tis since the nuptial of Lucentio,
     Come Pentecost as quickly as it will,                35
     Some five and twenty years, and then we masked.
COUSIN CAPULET  'Tis more, 'tis more, his son is elder, sir;
     His son is thirty.
CAPULET            Will you tell me that?
     His son was but a ward two years ago.
ROMEO  [*To a Servingman*] What lady's that which doth enrich the
        hand                40
     Of yonder knight?
SERVINGMAN  I know not, sir.

*Romeo is entranced by Juliet's beauty. Tybalt, recognising Romeo's voice, is outraged that a Montague should dare gatecrash Capulet's party. Capulet scolds Tybalt for wanting to pick a fight.*

## 1 Love at first sight (in groups of four or five)

Do you believe in love at first sight? Romeo loves Juliet from the first moment he sees her. She falls instantly in love with him. Talk together about what happens in that electrifying moment when two people fall head over heels in love. Then take the title 'Love at first sight' and make up and perform a short play, or write a short story, or draw a cartoon strip. See if you can end your play, story or cartoon with the line 'For I ne'er saw true beauty till this night'.

## 2 Tybalt and Capulet – single words
(in groups of five or six)

Capulet simply won't put up with Tybalt's intention to pick a fight at the party. Try the following exercise. It will help you to understand the characters of the two men.

Read, in turn, lines 53–91, one or two lines at a time. Then read aloud, just one word from each line. Don't worry about the meaning. When your turn comes, simply say whatever word strikes you as being the most important in the line – for any reason.

Repeat the exercise several times, with a different person starting at line 53 each time. Talk together about whether you think there are 'typical' Tybalt words, and 'typical' Capulet words, and what they suggest about the character of each.

**Ethiop** Elizabethans used this word for any black African
**measure** dance
**antic face** fantastic mask
**fleer** sneer

**portly** dignified
**goodman** not a gentleman (so 'goodman boy' would be a double insult to Tybalt)

ROMEO O she doth teach the torches to burn bright!
   It seems she hangs upon the cheek of night
   As a rich jewel in an Ethiop's ear –      45
   Beauty too rich for use, for earth too dear:
   So shows a snowy dove trooping with crows,
   As yonder lady o'er her fellows shows.
   The measure done, I'll watch her place of stand,
   And touching hers, make blessèd my rude hand.   50
   Did my heart love till now? forswear it, sight!
   For I ne'er saw true beauty till this night.
TYBALT This, by his voice, should be a Montague.
   Fetch me my rapier, boy.
              [*Exit Page*]
         What dares the slave
   Come hither, covered with an antic face,     55
   To fleer and scorn at our solemnity?
   Now by the stock and honour of my kin,
   To strike him dead I hold it not a sin.
CAPULET Why, how now, kinsman, wherefore storm you so?
TYBALT Uncle, this is a Montague, our foe:     60
   A villain that is hither come in spite,
   To scorn at our solemnity this night.
CAPULET Young Romeo is it?
TYBALT        'Tis he, that villain Romeo.
CAPULET Content thee, gentle coz, let him alone,
   'A bears him like a portly gentleman;     65
   And to say truth, Verona brags of him
   To be a virtuous and well-governed youth.
   I would not for the wealth of all this town
   Here in my house do him disparagement;
   Therefore be patient, take no note of him;   70
   It is my will, the which if thou respect,
   Show a fair presence, and put off these frowns,
   An ill-beseeming semblance for a feast.
TYBALT It fits when such a villain is a guest:
   I'll not endure him.
CAPULET       He shall be endured.   75
   What, goodman boy, I say he shall, go to!
   Am I the master here, or you? go to!
   You'll not endure him? God shall mend my soul,

*Tybalt, rebuked by Capulet, leaves the party. He threatens vengeance. Romeo and Juliet talk together for the first time. Romeo learns from the Nurse that Juliet is a Capulet.*

## 1 The first meeting of the lovers (in pairs)

It's helpful to know several things about lines 92–105:

- they are written as a sonnet
- sonnet writing was a popular and highly esteemed activity at Queen Elizabeth's court (see page 211)
- pilgrims, to show their faith, made long journeys to the shrines of the Holy Land. They brought back palm leaves as proof of their visits, and so were known as 'palmers'.
- Romeo compares Juliet to a shrine or saint. Religious imagery runs through their conversation (profane, holy shrine, sin, pilgrims, wrong, devotion, palmers, faith, despair, purged, trespass).

Sit facing each other, one as Romeo, one as Juliet. Read your lines slowly, pointing at yourself or your partner (or your own or your partner's hands or lips) on each appropriate mention. Use your imagination to perform actions you feel are appropriate to the words.

Afterwards, talk with your partner about this first meeting of Romeo and Juliet. For example, discuss:

- why you think Romeo uses this religious imagery
- how Romeo's language is different from how he's spoken earlier
- whether you feel he's now genuinely in love
- how you think Juliet feels on this first meeting.

**princox** cocky youngster
**choler** anger
**gall** poison
**palmer** pilgrim (see above)
**Marry** By St Mary (a mild oath)

You'll make a mutiny among my guests!

You will set cock-a-hoop! you'll be the man!          80

TYBALT Why, uncle, 'tis a shame.

CAPULET                    Go to, go to,

You are a saucy boy. Is't so indeed?

This trick may chance to scathe you, I know what.

You must contrary me! Marry, 'tis time. –

Well said, my hearts! – You are a princox, go,          85

Be quiet, or – More light, more light! – For shame,

I'll make you quiet, what! – Cheerly, my hearts!

TYBALT Patience perforce with wilful choler meeting

Makes my flesh tremble in their different greeting:

I will withdraw, but this intrusion shall,          90

Now seeming sweet, convert to bitt'rest gall.          *Exit*

ROMEO [*To Juliet*] If I profane with my unworthiest hand

This holy shrine, the gentle sin is this,

My lips, two blushing pilgrims, ready stand

To smooth that rough touch with a tender kiss.          95

JULIET Good pilgrim, you do wrong your hand too much,

Which mannerly devotion shows in this,

For saints have hands that pilgrims' hands do touch,

And palm to palm is holy palmers' kiss.

ROMEO Have not saints lips, and holy palmers too?          100

JULIET Ay, pilgrim, lips that they must use in prayer.

ROMEO O then, dear saint, let lips do what hands do:

They pray, grant thou, lest faith turn to despair.

JULIET Saints do not move, though grant for prayers' sake.

ROMEO Then move not while my prayer's effect I take.          105

Thus from my lips, by thine, my sin is purged.

[*Kissing her.*]

JULIET Then have my lips the sin that they have took.

ROMEO Sin from my lips? O trespass sweetly urged!

Give me my sin again.

[*Kissing her again.*]

JULIET                    You kiss by th'book.

NURSE Madam, your mother craves a word with you.          110

ROMEO What is her mother?

NURSE                    Marry, bachelor,

Her mother is the lady of the house,

And a good lady, and a wise and virtuous.

*Romeo realises with dismay that Juliet is a Capulet. The party ends and Juliet feels similar foreboding on learning Romeo's name. She has fallen in love with one of her family's hated enemies.*

## 1 Excuses (in groups of four or five)

The stage direction 'They whisper in his ear' means that Romeo and his masked friends say something to Capulet. Talk together about what they might have said that makes Capulet reply as he does. Then act out the stage direction to the class, letting them hear what you tell Capulet.

## 2 Finding out names (in pairs)

Juliet wants to find out Romeo's name, but does it indirectly. Improvise with your partner a sequence called 'finding out your lover's name – without showing you are interested!'

## 3 'My grave is like to be my wedding bed'

This is the first time Juliet speaks in such a sombre mood, imagining Death as her bridegroom. You'll find, as you read on, that this image of Death marrying Juliet keeps appearing in the play (see page 84). Make a sketch to illustrate the line.

## 4 'My only love sprung from my only hate!'

Have you heard an echo of this earlier in the play?

## 5 What movements? (in pairs)

Work out the Nurse's gestures for lines 115–16. You'll find quite a number of possibilities.

---

**the chinks** rattle a handful of coins
  to hear why the Nurse says this
**dear account** terrible reckoning
**fay** faith
**prodigious** ominous, monstrous

       I nursed her daughter that you talked withal;
       I tell you, he that can lay hold of her            115
       Shall have the chinks.
ROMEO                Is she a Capulet?
       O dear account! my life is my foe's debt.
BENVOLIO Away, be gone, the sport is at the best.
ROMEO Ay, so I fear, the more is my unrest.
CAPULET Nay, gentlemen, prepare not to be gone,     120
       We have a trifling foolish banquet towards.
               [*They whisper in his ear.*]
       Is it e'en so? Why then I thank you all.
       I thank you, honest gentlemen, good night.
       More torches here, come on! then let's to bed.
       Ah, sirrah, by my fay, it waxes late,          125
       I'll to my rest.
             [*Exeunt all but Juliet and Nurse*]
JULIET Come hither, Nurse. What is yond gentleman?
NURSE The son and heir of old Tiberio.
JULIET What's he that now is going out of door?
NURSE Marry, that I think be young Petruchio.     130
JULIET What's he that follows here, that would not dance?
NURSE I know not.
JULIET Go ask his name. – If he be marrièd,
       My grave is like to be my wedding bed.
NURSE His name is Romeo, and a Montague,      135
       The only son of your great enemy.
JULIET My only love sprung from my only hate!
       Too early seen ùnknown, and known too late!
       Prodigious birth of love it is to me,
       That I must love a loathèd enemy.          140
NURSE What's tis? what's tis?
JULIET               A rhyme I learnt even now
       Of one I danced withal.
           *One calls within,* 'Juliet!'
NURSE              Anon, anon!
       Come let's away, the strangers all are gone.
                          *Exeunt*

# Looking back at Act 1
*Activities for groups or individuals*

## 1 What kind of city is Verona?

Design a stage set to show your idea of Verona. Will it have towers, battlements, turrets, balconies? How can you create the narrow, threatening alleys of the old town, the large public spaces, the grand mansions of the Capulets and Montagues with their secluded orchards and high walls?

Draw a street map of Verona showing where the characters live. Where is 'Old Free-town', where Prince Escales sat in judgement?

## 2 Cast the play

You are a director about to film the play. Who would you sign up to play some of the characters you've met so far? Choose anyone you like: film or television actors, singers or other public figures. Say why you think each is suitable. You might try casting the play from the teachers in your school or college – or from among your fellow students. Remember, Juliet is only thirteen!

## 3 What's happened so far? Headlines

Imagine you are a newspaper sub-editor. Is your paper a tabloid or a 'heavy'? Your job is to write brief, memorable headlines for each of the five scenes of Act 1. Make your five headlines as accurate as possible. Try to use some of Shakespeare's own words.

## 4 Rosaline's diary

Until he sees Juliet, Romeo believes he is in love with Rosaline. Write a few entries in Rosaline's diary. How does she feel about Romeo's infatuation? What did she say as she kept him at a distance (see 1.1.199–215), refusing his advances? Remember, she is Juliet's cousin, so she's a Capulet too.

## 5 An agony aunt advises Romeo – something to write

Benvolio tells Romeo that the cure for his infatuation is to look at other girls ('Examine other beauties'). Imagine you are an 'agony aunt' for a magazine. Romeo writes to you with his problem (using the language of the play 1.1.154–227). Write his letter and your advice.

## 6 The television reporter at the Capulet party – updating the play

Shakespeare's Verona certainly didn't have television! But don't be afraid to explore the play using your experience of television.

You have been sent by a television station to report on Capulet's party (Scene 5). Your news editor says 'Don't forget to interview the servants – they're the ones who will really know! And I've heard that the lively Helena is a real chatterbox! You'll be given a two-minute 'slot', no more, in tomorrow's *News.*'

Prepare and deliver your report.

## 7 Tybalt's point of view

Tybalt meets his friends as he leaves Capulet's party. Tell the story he tells them of the party and his past experience of the Montagues. Can you capture Tybalt's tone and language?

## 8 Married at thirteen?

Lady Capulet urges thirteen-year-old Juliet to marry. Talk together about the reasons she uses for marrying so young. What do you think of the idea of getting married at thirteen? . . . and how old is Romeo?

## 9 A letter from Verona

Imagine you are a member of either the Montague or Capulet household. Write a letter to your cousins in Mantua describing what's happened so far. Some events you've taken part in, but you only know other things through eavesdropping or gossip. Your cousins in Mantua are eager for news and you don't wish to disappoint them!

## 10 Friendships

What makes Romeo, Mercutio and Benvolio close friends? Talk together about what they have in common and in what ways they are different. Also talk about Tybalt and his group of unnamed friends. What binds them together?

Think about how you choose your own friends and how Romeo's and Tybalt's friends are like teenage groups today. Why do you think Juliet doesn't seem to have any friends of her own age?

Romeo and Juliet

*Chorus reminds the audience that Romeo's infatuation with Rosaline has ended. Romeo now loves Juliet, who returns his love. But dangers beset the young lovers. Act 2 begins with Mercutio teasing the hidden Romeo.*

## 1 Chorus (in groups of four to seven)

Sit in a circle. Read Chorus' speech, each person reading a line in turn. Then talk together about some of the following:

a All companies acting Shakespeare 'double' the parts (actors play more than one role). So Chorus is spoken by someone with another role (or roles) in the play. Look at the cast list on page 1 and decide who seems most likely to 'double' Chorus.

b Quite often these fourteen lines are cut in performance. Imagine you are a group preparing to put on the play. Half of you want to include Chorus' fourteen lines, half don't. Debate whether they should be left in or cut.

c Which line most appeals to the group? Prepare and show a tableau of the line. Can the other groups guess your line?

d Act out the story so far. The words of Chorus summarise much of the play so far. One person reads a line or two, then pauses. In that pause, other members of the group mime what is described. Two reminders: 'old desire' of line 144 is Rosaline; the last two lines imply that the pleasures of Romeo and Juliet's meetings make their hardships bearable.

## 2 'Nay, I'll conjure too' (in pairs)

Mercutio pretends to be a magician, raising up spirits. Imagine you are a director, and Mercutio has asked you what actions should accompany line 7. Talk together about how you think Mercutio should deliver the five words.

---

**again** in return
**temp'ring extremities** easing
 dangers
**dull earth** body

[*Enter*] CHORUS.

Now old desire doth in his death-bed lie,
And young affection gapes to be his heir;                           145
That fair for which love groaned for and would die,
With tender Juliet matched is now not fair.
Now Romeo is beloved, and loves again,
Alike bewitchèd by the charm of looks;
But to his foe supposed he must complain,                           150
And she steal love's sweet bait from fearful hooks.
Being held a foe, he may not have access
To breathe such vows as lovers use to swear,
And she as much in love, her means much less
To meet her new-belovèd any where:                                  155
But passion lends them power, time means, to meet,
Temp'ring extremities with extreme sweet.            [*Exit*]


ACT 2   SCENE 1
Outside Capulet's mansion


Enter ROMEO alone.

ROMEO Can I go forward when my heart is here?
    Turn back, dull earth, and find thy centre out.
                                    [*Romeo withdraws*]

*Enter* BENVOLIO *with* MERCUTIO.

BENVOLIO Romeo! my cousin Romeo! Romeo!
MERCUTIO                              He is wise,
    And on my life hath stol'n him home to bed.
BENVOLIO He ran this way and leapt this orchard wall.       5
    Call, good Mercutio.
MERCUTIO                    Nay, I'll conjure too.
    Romeo! humours! madman! passion! lover!
    Appear thou in the likeness of a sigh,

*Mercutio, pretending to be a magician, uses much sexual innuendo as he mocks Romeo's love for Rosaline.*

## Playing with words

Mercutio teases Romeo, seizing every opportunity to make sexual puns:

*demesnes*　parklands for pleasure (or sexual parts)
*spirit*　ghost (or semen)
*circle*　magic circle (or vagina)
*stand*　ghost rising (or sexual erection)
*down*　ghost disappearing (or end of sexual intercourse)
*honest*　proper (and virginal)
*mark*　target (or sexual intercourse)
*medlar*　apple-like fruit (or female sexual organ)
*open-arse*　slang for medlar (or female sexual organ)
*pop'rin pear*　pear from Poperinghe in Flanders (shaped like a penis)

As you read through the play look out for more examples of Mercutio's word-play. Why do you think Shakespeare makes Mercutio talk in this way? Find examples on the opposite page where he uses puns (words with more than one meaning) that are not sexual.

'Her purblind son and heir, Young Abraham Cupid.' Look for other mentions in the play of blind, or blindfolded, Cupid shooting his love arrows at random.

**Venus** goddess of love
**Abraham** beggar, or old man, or famous archer

**King Cophetua** king who loved a poor girl (in an old ballad)
**truckle-bed** camp bed

Speak but one rhyme, and I am satisfied;
Cry but 'Ay me!', pronounce but 'love' and 'dove',                    10
Speak to my gossip Venus one fair word,
One nickname for her purblind son and heir,
Young Abraham Cupid, he that shot so trim
When King Cophetua loved the beggar-maid.
He heareth not, he stirreth not, he moveth not,                     15
The ape is dead, and I must conjure him.
I conjure thee by Rosaline's bright eyes,
By her high forehead and her scarlet lip,
By her fine foot, straight leg, and quivering thigh,
And the demesnes that there adjacent lie,                          20
That in thy likeness thou appear to us.
BENVOLIO And if he hear thee, thou wilt anger him.
MERCUTIO This cannot anger him; 'twould anger him
          To raise a spirit in his mistress' circle,
          Of some strange nature, letting it there stand          25
          Till she had laid it and conjured it down:
          That were some spite. My invocation
          Is fair and honest: in his mistress' name
          I conjure only but to raise up him.
BENVOLIO Come, he hath hid himself among these trees              30
          To be consorted with the humorous night:
          Blind is his love, and best befits the dark.
MERCUTIO If love be blind, love cannot hit the mark.
          Now will he sit under a medlar tree,
          And wish his mistress were that kind of fruit            35
          As maids call medlars, when they laugh alone.
          O Romeo, that she were, O that she were
          An open-arse, thou a pop'rin pear!
          Romeo, good night, I'll to my truckle-bed,
          This field-bed is too cold for me to sleep.              40
          Come, shall we go?
BENVOLIO                    Go then, for 'tis in vain
          To seek him here that means not to be found.
                                        *Exit* [*with Mercutio*]

*Romeo, hidden from Juliet, sees her at an upstairs window. He compares her to the sun, stars and heavens.*

---

## 1 Read through! (in pairs)

This scene is one of the most famous in all world drama. Probably the best way into it is simply to read it straight through, one person as Romeo, the other as Juliet. If you can find an upstairs window for Juliet, so much the better! Don't pause to discuss. Just go right through to line 189 on page 63. Enjoy yourselves!

## 2 Echoing the words (in pairs)

Echoing will help you to make discoveries about Romeo's language. Take lines 1–32. Sit facing each other. One student reads the lines aloud. The other listens (or follows in the script) and quietly echoes certain words: (a) all words to do with light or brightness or eyesight, and (b) all the words that refer to something overhead.

As you echo each 'upward' word, point your finger upward.

When you have completed both of these echoing exercises, talk together about what you think those 'light-giving' words and 'upward' words tell you about Romeo's feelings.

## 3 'He jests at scars that never felt a wound'
(in groups of three to six)

Make up a short play with line 1 as its title.

---

**vestal livery** virginal uniform (the moon was seen as Diana, goddess of virginity)
**sick and green** 'greensickness' was thought to be an illness of virgins

**spheres** orbits (the Ptolemaic system of astronomy held that the planets circled the earth. Their orbits (paths) were believed to be crystal spheres enclosing the earth)

# ACT 2   SCENE 2
## Capulet's orchard

ROMEO *advances.*

ROMEO  He jests at scars that never felt a wound.
　　　　But soft, what light through yonder window breaks?
　　　　It is the east, and Juliet is the sun.
　　　　Arise, fair sun, and kill the envious moon,
　　　　Who is already sick and pale with grief　　　　　　5
　　　　That thou, her maid, art far more fair than she.
　　　　Be not her maid, since she is envious;
　　　　Her vestal livery is but sick and green,
　　　　And none but fools do wear it; cast it off.

　　　　[JULIET *appears aloft as at a window.*]

　　　　It is my lady, O it is my love:　　　　　　　　　　10
　　　　O that she knew she were!
　　　　She speaks, yet she says nothing; what of that?
　　　　Her eye discourses, I will answer it.
　　　　I am too bold, 'tis not to me she speaks:
　　　　Two of the fairest stars in all the heaven,　　　　15
　　　　Having some business, do entreat her eyes
　　　　To twinkle in their spheres till they return.
　　　　What if her eyes were there, they in her head?
　　　　The brightness of her cheek would shame those stars,
　　　　As daylight doth a lamp; her eyes in heaven　　20
　　　　Would through the airy region stream so bright
　　　　That birds would sing and think it were not night.
　　　　See how she leans her cheek upon her hand!
　　　　O that I were a glove upon that hand,
　　　　That I might touch that cheek!
JULIET　　　　　　　　　　　　　　Ay me!
ROMEO [*Aside*]　　　　　　　　　　　　She speaks.　　25
　　　　O speak again, bright angel, for thou art
　　　　As glorious to this night, being o'er my head,
　　　　As is a wingèd messenger of heaven
　　　　Unto the white-upturnèd wond'ring eyes

*Juliet declares her love for Romeo in spite of his belonging to the hated Montagues. When Romeo reveals himself she fears for his safety.*

What's in a name? When Juliet asks 'Wherefore art thou Romeo?' she begins to question why her love should be named Romeo – a hated Montague! It's the name that is the trouble, not Romeo himself. The word, not the person.

## 1 ''Tis but thy name that is my enemy' (in groups of three)

Make a list of some groups that are regarded by others as 'enemies', like the Montagues and the Capulets. Talk together about what would happen if a girl and boy from each opposing group fell in love.

## 2 'That which we call a rose
## By any other word would smell as sweet'
(in groups of five or six)

So why do we call a rose a rose? Improvise what would happen if you went around calling things by different names (e.g. try calling 'school' 'restaurant', and so on). And what would happen if you decided you should be called by a quite different name? Choose a new name, perhaps from a different ethnic group, and talk together about what would happen if you insisted on being called that new name at home, at school and elsewhere.

## 3 Echoing 'names' (in pairs)

One person reads aloud lines 33–61. The other echoes every time 'name' is mentioned, or a proper name (e.g. Capulet), or any similar word (e.g. 'called').

When you've tried one or more of the activities, talk together about how important you think names are. Could we simply re-name people and things, throwing away the 'old' names? Would changing names make the world a better place?

---

**wherefore** why
**owes** owns
**doff** cast off

                    Of mortals that fall back to gaze on him,                    30
                    When he bestrides the lazy puffing clouds,
                    And sails upon the bosom of the air.
JULIET  O Romeo, Romeo, wherefore art thou Romeo?
                    Deny thy father and refuse thy name;
                    Or if thou wilt not, be but sworn my love,                    35
                    And I'll no longer be a Capulet.
ROMEO  [*Aside*] Shall I hear more, or shall I speak at this?
JULIET  'Tis but thy name that is my enemy;
                    Thou art thyself, though not a Montague.
                    What's Montague? It is nor hand nor foot,                    40
                    Nor arm nor face, nor any other part
                    Belonging to a man. O be some other name!
                    What's in a name? That which we call a rose
                    By any other word would smell as sweet;
                    So Romeo would, were he not Romeo called,                    45
                    Retain that dear perfection which he owes
                    Without that title. Romeo, doff thy name,
                    And for thy name, which is no part of thee,
                    Take all myself.
ROMEO                         I take thee at thy word:
                    Call me but love, and I'll be new baptised;                    50
                    Henceforth I never will be Romeo.
JULIET  What man art thou that thus bescreened in night
                    So stumblest on my counsel?
ROMEO                               By a name
                    I know not how to tell thee who I am.
                    My name, dear saint, is hateful to myself,                    55
                    Because it is an enemy to thee;
                    Had I it written, I would tear the word.
JULIET  My ears have yet not drunk a hundred words
                    Of thy tongue's uttering, yet I know the sound.
                    Art thou not Romeo, and a Montague?                    60
ROMEO  Neither, fair maid, if either thee dislike.
JULIET  How cam'st thou hither, tell me, and wherefore?
                    The orchard walls are high and hard to climb,
                    And the place death, considering who thou art,
                    If any of my kinsmen find thee here.                    65
ROMEO  With love's light wings did I o'erperch these walls,
                    For stony limits cannot hold love out,

*Juliet warns Romeo that her family will kill him if they find him. Admitting embarrassment at being overheard telling of her love, she asks if he loves her.*

## 1 Juliet's language (in groups of four or five)

Juliet's 'fain would I dwell on form' suggests she would gladly stick to formality and ceremonial politeness. But her 'farewell compliment' (line 89) shows her rejecting stiff, customary ways of behaving and speaking. To find if she succeeds in her wish to speak simply and truly, without affectation, try this: sit in a circle, and read lines 90–106 ('Dost thou love me? . . . discovered'). The first group member begins, but reads only to a punctuation mark (full stop, comma, etc.). The second group member then reads to the next punctuation mark, and stops. The third does the same, and so on round the group. Read the lines three times in this way.

After the readings, talk together about Juliet's language, especially how you think it is different from the language of all the men who have spoken in the play. Find examples of where she speaks without formality. Talk about how different you think her way of speaking is from how a girl would speak today.

## 2 Romeo's language – can you make it physical? (in pairs)

Sit facing each other. One reads all Romeo's lines opposite. Read slowly, a little at a time. The other mimes a gesture for each of Romeo's thoughts or images. Then change roles. Afterwards, discuss the images Romeo uses in these twelve lines. Talk together about how you think the images he uses reflect the themes of the play (see pages 204–06).

**prorogued** postponed
**fain** gladly
**perjuries** lies
**Jove** Jupiter, god of oaths (who did not take lovers' vows seriously!)

**fond** foolish
**coying to be strange** cunning to be distant or offhand

And what love can do, that dares love attempt:
Therefore thy kinsmen are no stop to me.

JULIET  If they do see thee, they will murder thee.                    70

ROMEO  Alack, there lies more peril in thine eye
Than twenty of their swords. Look thou but sweet,
And I am proof against their enmity.

JULIET  I would not for the world they saw thee here.

ROMEO  I have night's cloak to hide me from their eyes,            75
And but thou love me, let them find me here;
My life were better ended by their hate,
Than death proroguèd, wanting of thy love.

JULIET  By whose direction found'st thou out this place?

ROMEO  By Love, that first did prompt me to enquire:               80
He lent me counsel, and I lent him eyes.
I am no pilot, yet wert thou as far
As that vast shore washed with the farthest sea,
I should adventure for such merchandise.

JULIET  Thou knowest the mask of night is on my face,            85
Else would a maiden blush bepaint my cheek
For that which thou hast heard me speak tonight.
Fain would I dwell on form, fain, fain deny
What I have spoke, but farewell compliment.
Dost thou love me? I know thou wilt say 'Ay';               90
And I will take thy word; yet if thou swear'st,
Thou mayst prove false: at lovers' perjuries
They say Jove laughs. O gentle Romeo,
If thou dost love, pronounce it faithfully;
Or if thou think'st I am too quickly won,                   95
I'll frown and be perverse, and say thee nay,
So thou wilt woo, but else not for the world.
In truth, fair Montague, I am too fond,
And therefore thou mayst think my behaviour light:
But trust me, gentleman, I'll prove more true              100
Than those that have more coying to be strange.
I should have been more strange, I must confess,
But that thou overheard'st, ere I was ware,
My true-love passion; therefore pardon me,
And not impute this yielding to light love,                105
Which the dark night hath so discoverèd.

*Romeo and Juliet exchange vows of love, but both are fearful. Juliet fears the suddenness of their love. Romeo fears because it seems dream-like and unreal.*

Royal Shakespeare Theatre, 1961. What line is being spoken at this moment do you think?

## 1 'Too like the lightning' (lines 118–20)

Shakespeare probably wrote *A Midsummer Night's Dream* at about the same time (1595) as *Romeo and Juliet*. In that play two other young lovers are also beset with problems. Lysander uses the same image as Juliet. He compares love to the briefness of lightning:

'Swift as a shadow, short as any dream,
Brief as the lightning in the collied night
That in a spleen unfolds both heaven and earth,
And – ere a man hath power to say "Behold!" –
The jaws of darkness do devour it up.
So quick bright things come to confusion'.

Do you feel that 'lightning' is a fitting description or image of Romeo and Juliet's love?

**bounty** generosity, willingness to give

58

ROMEO  Lady, by yonder blessèd moon I vow,
       That tips with silver all these fruit-tree tops –
JULIET  O swear not by the moon, th'inconstant moon,
       That monthly changes in her circled orb,                    110
       Lest that thy love prove likewise variable.
ROMEO  What shall I swear by?
JULIET                         Do not swear at all;
       Or if thou wilt, swear by thy gracious self,
       Which is the god of my idolatry,
       And I'll believe thee.
ROMEO                         If my heart's dear love –            115
JULIET  Well, do not swear. Although I joy in thee,
       I have no joy of this contract tonight,
       It is too rash, too unadvised, too sudden,
       Too like the lightning, which doth cease to be
       Ere one can say 'It lightens'. Sweet, good night:          120
       This bud of love, by summer's ripening breath,
       May prove a beauteous flower when next we meet.
       Good night, good night! as sweet repose and rest
       Come to thy heart as that within my breast.
ROMEO  O wilt thou leave me so unsatisfied?                       125
JULIET  What satisfaction canst thou have tonight?
ROMEO  Th'exchange of thy love's faithful vow for mine.
JULIET  I gave thee mine before thou didst request it;
       And yet I would it were to give again.
ROMEO  Wouldst thou withdraw it? for what purpose, love?         130
JULIET  But to be frank and give it thee again,
       And yet I wish but for the thing I have:
       My bounty is as boundless as the sea,
       My love as deep; the more I give to thee
       The more I have, for both are infinite.                    135
              [*Nurse calls within.*]
       I hear some noise within; dear love, adieu! –
       Anon, good Nurse! – Sweet Montague, be true.
       Stay but a little, I will come again.          [*Exit above*]
ROMEO  O blessèd, blessèd night! I am afeard,
       Being in night, all this is but a dream,                   140
       Too flattering-sweet to be substantial.

*Juliet, promising marriage, says she will send a messenger tomorrow to ask the time and place of the wedding. At the Nurse's call, Juliet goes inside the house. Returning, she calls Romeo back.*

### 1 'O for a falc 'ner's voice'

Falconry (hunting with birds of prey) was a popular sport of the Elizabethans. The falconer, or huntsman, used a lure (or bait) and a special call to bring the bird back to the captivity of his hand.

Juliet likens Romeo to a 'tassel-gentle' (line 159), a male peregrine falcon, the bird of princes. Later (line 167), Romeo calls Juliet his 'niësse' (a young unfledged hawk). Use the library to find out more about falconry. Explore how that knowledge can help your understanding of the play.

### 2 'As schoolboys from their books' (in groups of four)

Whenever Shakespeare mentions school, he seems less than enthusiastic about it. Try this one-minute exercise!

Show in a tableau, what you think Shakespeare had in mind when he gave these words to Romeo (line 156). Hold your freeze for thirty seconds. Try the same exercise with line 157.

### 3 'I have forgot why I did call thee back'

If you were directing the play, could you make the audience laugh at this moment (line 170)? Would you wish to make them laugh?

---

**bent** intention
**cease thy strife** stop your effort (of loving me)
**bondage is hoarse** prisoners must whisper

**Echo** a cave-dwelling nymph, in love with Narcissus. She repeated the last word anyone spoke to her. Echo wasted away until only her voice remained

*[Enter Juliet above.]*

JULIET  Three words, dear Romeo, and good night indeed.
    If that thy bent of love be honourable,
    Thy purpose marriage, send me word tomorrow,
    By one that I'll procure to come to thee,                    145
    Where and what time thou wilt perform the rite,
    And all my fortunes at thy foot I'll lay,
    And follow thee my lord throughout the world.
NURSE  *[Within]* Madam!
JULIET  I come, anon. – But if thou meanest not well,            150
    I do beseech thee –
NURSE  *[Within]*              Madam!
JULIET                              By and by I come –
    To cease thy strife, and leave me to my grief.
    Tomorrow will I send.
ROMEO  So thrive my soul –
JULIET                    A thousand times good night!
                                        *[Exit above]*
ROMEO  A thousand times the worse, to want thy light.           155
    Love goes toward love as schoolboys from their books,
    But love from love, toward school with heavy looks.
                    *[Retiring slowly.]*

                *Enter Juliet again [above].*

JULIET  Hist, Romeo, hist! O for a falc'ner's voice,
    To lure this tassel-gentle back again:
    Bondage is hoarse, and may not speak aloud,                 160
    Else would I tear the cave where Echo lies,
    And make her airy tongue more hoarse than mine
    With repetition of my Romeo's name.
ROMEO  It is my soul that calls upon my name.
    How silver-sweet sound lovers' tongues by night,           165
    Like softest music to attending ears!
JULIET  Romeo!
ROMEO        My nïesse?
JULIET                    What a'clock tomorrow
    Shall I send to thee?
ROMEO                    By the hour of nine.
JULIET  I will not fail, 'tis twenty year till then.
    I have forgot why I did call thee back.                     170

*Romeo and Juliet reluctantly part. She compares him to a captive bird.*
*Romeo promises to seek Friar Lawrence's help.*

## 1 Moods and sincerity (in pairs)

Look back over lines 1–189 and trace the changing moods of the two
lovers. Can you identify those lines where you feel they are truly
speaking from the heart?

You will often hear Juliet's 'parting is such sweet sorrow' (line 184)
spoken today. Can you find other familiar sayings in the play (see page
210)?

Learn by heart a few of the lines that especially appeal to you in this
scene.

## 2 Work out your own staging of the scene
   (in pairs or threes)

Where might the scene be played: the stage in the school hall the
drama studio, the Globe Theatre (see page 214), in the open air
somewhere in the school grounds? Choose the space you prefer.
Make drawings to show where Romeo and Juliet will be at key
moments. It's worth remembering that although this is usually called
'the balcony scene', Shakespeare doesn't mention a balcony. So
decide how you wish to act the stage direction 'Juliet appears aloft as
at a window'.

Best of all, act out the scene in your chosen space.

**wanton's bird** spoilt child's pet
  bird (held captive by string tied to
  its legs)
**gyves** fetters on the legs of
  prisoners

**ghostly sire** Friar Lawrence
  (Romeo's 'spiritual father')
**close cell** private room
**dear hap** good fortune

ROMEO   Let me stand here till thou remember it.

JULIET   I shall forget, to have thee still stand there,
        Rememb'ring how I love thy company.

ROMEO   And I'll still stay, to have thee still forget,
        Forgetting any other home but this.                              175

JULIET   'Tis almost morning, I would have thee gone:
        And yet no farther than a wanton's bird,
        That lets it hop a little from his hand,
        Like a poor prisoner in his twisted gyves,
        And with a silken thread plucks it back again,            180
        So loving-jealous of his liberty.

ROMEO   I would I were thy bird.

JULIET                    Sweet, so would I,
        Yet I should kill thee with much cherishing.
        Good night, good night! Parting is such sweet sorrow,
        That I shall say good night till it be morrow.   [*Exit above*]   185

ROMEO   Sleep dwell upon thine eyes, peace in thy breast!
        Would I were sleep and peace, so sweet to rest!
        Hence will I to my ghostly sire's close cell,
        His help to crave, and my dear hap to tell.               *Exit*

*At daybreak, Friar Lawrence is gathering flowers and herbs. He reflects that, like people, they contain both healing medicine and poison, both good and evil.*

Can you identify an appropriate line? Leo McKern as Friar Lawrence, Shakespeare Memorial Theatre 1954.

## 1 Friar Lawrence: what's he like?
(in groups of four or five)

This is the first time we meet Friar Lawrence. He will play a vital part in what happens to Romeo and Juliet.

Read lines 1–30 around the group, each person reading two lines before handing on to the next person.

Notice all the opposing contrasts he makes: 'smiles/frowning', 'day/night', 'baleful weeds/precious-juiced flowers', 'mother/tomb', 'grave/womb', 'vile/good', 'fair use/abuse', 'virtue/vice', 'poison/medicine', 'cheers/stays', 'grace/rude will'. Talk together about how these oppositions help your understanding of the play (you will find help on pages 204–06).

## 2 Echoing (in pairs)

One person reads, slowly, lines 5–30. The other person says either 'life' or 'death' whenever they hear words that have those implications. The oppositions listed above will help you.

---

**Titan** Helios, the sun god, who drove his blazing chariot (the sun) across the sky
**osier cage** willow basket
**baleful** evil or poisonous
**divers** many

**mickle** great
**strained** diverted
**stays** kills
**grace and rude will** divine virtue and human passions

# ACT 2   SCENE 3
## Outside Friar Lawrence's cell

*Enter* FRIAR LAWRENCE *alone, with a basket.*

FRIAR LAWRENCE

The grey-eyed morn smiles on the frowning night,
Check'ring the eastern clouds with streaks of light;
And fleckled darkness like a drunkard reels
From forth day's path and Titan's fiery wheels:
Now ere the sun advance his burning eye,                    5
The day to cheer, and night's dank dew to dry,
I must upfill this osier cage of ours
With baleful weeds and precious-juicèd flowers.
The earth that's nature's mother is her tomb;
What is her burying grave, that is her womb;               10
And from her womb children of divers kind
We sucking on her natural bosom find:
Many for many virtues excellent,
None but for some, and yet all different.
O mickle is the powerful grace that lies                   15
In plants, herbs, stones, and their true qualities:
For nought so vile, that on the earth doth live,
But to the earth some special good doth give;
Nor ought so good but, strained from that fair use,
Revolts from true birth, stumbling on abuse.               20
Virtue itself turns vice, being misapplied,
And vice sometime by action dignified.

*Enter* ROMEO.

Within the infant rind of this weak flower
Poison hath residence, and medicine power:
For this, being smelt, with that part cheers each part,    25
Being tasted, stays all senses with the heart.
Two such opposèd kings encamp them still
In man as well as herbs, grace and rude will;
And where the worser is predominant,
Full soon the canker death eats up that plant.            30

65

*Friar Lawrence fears that Romeo has spent the night with Rosaline. But Romeo, telling of his and Juliet's mutual love, asks the Friar to marry them.*

---

## 1 'Riddling confession finds but riddling shrift' (in pairs)

Friar Lawrence doesn't find Romeo's explanation (lines 48–54) at all clear. He tells Romeo that ambiguous, unclear confessions will only be given similarly unsatisfactory absolution ('riddling shrift'). As a Franciscan priest, Friar Lawrence could give absolution (shrift, pardon, forgiveness) to those who confessed (told him of) their sins.

To clarify Romeo's explanation, try this activity. One person reads lines 48–54. But only read up to a punctuation mark, then pause. The other person, in each pause, makes clear Romeo's veiled (riddling) meaning.

## 2 'Rich Capulet' – something to think about

Why do you think Romeo calls Capulet 'rich'?

## 3 Rhyme

Read the last word in each line aloud. What do you discover? Find out if the whole scene is written in this way.

---

**Benedicite!** Bless you!
**distemp'rature** troubled mind
**ghostly** spiritual (priestly)

**holy physic** religious medicine (the marriage ceremony)
**intercession** entreaty or request
**steads** benefits

ROMEO Good morrow, father.
FRIAR LAWRENCE                    Benedicite!
          What early tongue so sweet saluteth me?
          Young son, it argues a distempered head
          So soon to bid good morrow to thy bed:
          Care keeps his watch in every old man's eye,                    35
          And where care lodges, sleep will never lie;
          But where unbruisèd youth with unstuffed brain
          Doth couch his limbs, there golden sleep doth reign.
          Therefore thy earliness doth me assure
          Thou art uproused with some distemp'rature;                    40
          Or if not so, then here I hit it right,
          Our Romeo hath not been in bed tonight.
ROMEO That last is true, the sweeter rest was mine.
FRIAR LAWRENCE God pardon sin! wast thou with Rosaline?
ROMEO With Rosaline, my ghostly father? no;                    45
          I have forgot that name, and that name's woe.
FRIAR LAWRENCE
          That's my good son, but where hast thou been then?
ROMEO I'll tell thee ere thou ask it me again:
          I have been feasting with mine enemy,
          Where on a sudden one hath wounded me                    50
          That's by me wounded; both our remedies
          Within thy help and holy physic lies.
          I bear no hatred, blessèd man; for lo,
          My intercession likewise steads my foe.
FRIAR LAWRENCE Be plain, good son, and homely in thy drift,                    55
          Riddling confession finds but riddling shrift.
ROMEO Then plainly know, my heart's dear love is set
          On the fair daughter of rich Capulet;
          As mine on hers, so hers is set on mine,
          And all combined, save what thou must combine                    60
          By holy marriage. When and where and how
          We met, we wooed, and made exchange of vow,
          I'll tell thee as we pass, but this I pray,
          That thou consent to marry us today.

*After chiding Romeo for his fickleness in love, Friar Lawrence agrees to marry Romeo and Juliet because he believes their marriage will end the feuding of the Montagues and Capulets.*

### 1 The last two lines (in pairs)

What do lines 93–4 suggest about the characters of Romeo and Friar Lawrence? Try reading a number of the speeches in the style that these last two lines suggest (Romeo: hasty; Friar Lawrence: wisely and slow). Talk together about whether you think those styles fit the language each character uses. Keep the idea of 'hasty/slow' in your mind as you read on.

### 2 Adult advice (in groups of four or five)

This scene shows a teenager telling an adult that he's in love. What would happen if you were in the same position? Improvise together a number of short examples of a modern teenager, like Romeo, head over heels in love with a new girl, talking with an adult (e.g. a priest, a teacher, a parent).

Work out what happens in each case. What does the adult say to the teenager?

### 3 'Thy love did read by rote, that could not spell'

In line 88, Friar Lawrence says Romeo's love for Rosaline was like mere recitation memorised from a book ('by rote'), without true understanding ('could not spell'). Look back through the earlier scenes of the play to see if you can find examples of Romeo's language that justify Friar Lawrence's claim.

---

**Holy Saint Francis** Friar
Lawrence is a Franciscan and
swears by the founder of his Order

**brine** salt water (tears)
**chid'st** chided, rebuked
**doting** infatuation

FRIAR LAWRENCE Holy Saint Francis, what a change is here!     65
    Is Rosaline, that thou didst love so dear,
    So soon forsaken? Young men's love then lies
    Not truly in their hearts, but in their eyes.
    Jesu Maria, what a deal of brine
    Hath washed thy sallow cheeks for Rosaline!     70
    How much salt water thrown away in waste,
    To season love, that of it doth not taste!
    The sun not yet thy sighs from heaven clears,
    Thy old groans yet ringing in mine ancient ears;
    Lo here upon thy cheek the stain doth sit     75
    Of an old tear that is not washed off yet.
    If e'er thou wast thyself, and these woes thine,
    Thou and these woes were all for Rosaline.
    And art thou changed? Pronounce this sentence then:
    Women may fall, when there's no strength in men.     80
ROMEO Thou chid'st me oft for loving Rosaline.
FRIAR LAWRENCE For doting, not for loving, pupil mine.
ROMEO And bad'st me bury love.
FRIAR LAWRENCE              Not in a grave,
    To lay one in, another out to have.
ROMEO I pray thee chide me not. Her I love now     85
    Doth grace for grace and love for love allow;
    The other did not so.
FRIAR LAWRENCE             O she knew well
    Thy love did read by rote, that could not spell.
    But come, young waverer, come go with me,
    In one respect I'll thy assistant be:     90
    For this alliance may so happy prove
    To turn your households' rancour to pure love.
ROMEO O let us hence, I stand on sudden haste.
FRIAR LAWRENCE Wisely and slow, they stumble that run fast.
                                           *Exeunt*

*Mercutio jokes with Benvolio about Tybalt's challenge to Romeo and about Romeo's infatuation with Rosaline. He mocks Tybalt's precise style of sword-fencing and the current fashions of speaking.*

These illustrations are from Italian fencing manuals published in the sixteenth century. Make your own drawings of the fencing movements that Mercutio names (passado = lunge; punto reverso = backhanded thrust; hay = hit).

**the very pin . . . bow-boy's butt-shaft** Romeo's heart has been pierced by Cupid's arrow
**Prince of Cats** Tybalt was a popular name for a cat

**prick-song** printed music (Mercutio makes an elaborate comparison between music and sword-fencing – both played precisely by the rules)
**affecting phantasimes** posturing young men

## ACT 2   SCENE 4
## A street in Verona

*Enter* BENVOLIO *and* MERCUTIO.

MERCUTIO  Where the dev'l should this Romeo be?
  Came he not home tonight?
BENVOLIO  Not to his father's, I spoke with his man.
MERCUTIO  Why, that same pale hard-hearted wench, that Rosaline,
  Torments him so, that he will sure run mad. 5
BENVOLIO  Tybalt, the kinsman to old Capulet,
  Hath sent a letter to his father's house.
MERCUTIO  A challenge, on my life.
BENVOLIO  Romeo will answer it.
MERCUTIO  Any man that can write may answer a letter. 10
BENVOLIO  Nay, he will answer the letter's master, how he dares, being
  dared.
MERCUTIO  Alas, poor Romeo, he is already dead, stabbed with a white
  wench's black eye, run through the ear with a love-song, the very
  pin of his heart cleft with the blind bow-boy's butt-shaft; and is 15
  he a man to encounter Tybalt?
BENVOLIO  Why, what is Tybalt?
MERCUTIO  More than Prince of Cats. O, he's the courageous captain
  of compliments: he fights as you sing prick-song, keeps time,
  distance, and proportion; he rests his minim rests, one, two, and 20
  the third in your bosom; the very butcher of a silk button, a duellist,
  a duellist; a gentleman of the very first house, of the first and second
  cause. Ah, the immortal 'passado', the 'punto reverso', the 'hay'!
BENVOLIO  The what?
MERCUTIO  The pox of such antic, lisping, affecting phantasimes, these 25
  new tuners of accent! 'By Jesu, a very good blade! a very tall man!
  a very good whore!' Why, is not this a lamentable thing, grandsire,
  that we should be thus afflicted with these strange flies, these
  fashion-mongers, these pardon-me's, who stand so much on the
  new form, that they cannot sit at ease on the old bench? O their 30
  bones, their bones!

Romeo and Juliet

*Mercutio (still thinking Romeo loves Rosaline) teases Romeo about his love. The two young men joke together, trying to outdo each other's puns.*

---

## 1 Mercutio's tragic ladies (in groups of six)

'Petrarch . . . Laura . . . Dido . . . Cleopatra . . . Helen and Hero . . . Thisbe'. Mercutio teases Romeo, accusing him of writing love poetry (numbers) to Rosaline like that of the fourteenth-century Italian poet Petrarch to his love, Laura. But all the examples he gives are ominous, because all ended tragically:

*Dido* queen of Carthage. When her lover Aeneas deserted her, she killed herself.

*Cleopatra* queen of Egypt, loved by both Julius Caesar and Mark Antony. She and Mark Antony committed suicide.

*Helen* wife of Menelaus, king of Sparta, was stolen by the Trojan Paris. Her abduction led to the siege and destruction of Troy.

*Hero* Every night her lover Leander swam across the Hellespont (the Dardanelles) to meet her. He drowned.

*Thisbe* loved Pyramus. Their families were bitter enemies. She could only speak to him through a chink in the wall between their houses.

Work out a short mime showing all the love stories.

## 2 Puns – something to think about

Mercutio obviously loves puns, particularly when he can add a sexual meaning (roe = sperm of fish *or* half of Romeo; slip = fake coin *or* escape; courtesy = bow *or* good manners; hit it = take the point *or* sexual intercourse; pink = perfection *or* a flower *or* decoration on a shoe; goose = bird *or* prostitute *or* nitwit). (See page 213)

## 3 What are they doing? (in pairs)

Act out lines 33–69, one as Romeo, one as Mercutio. You'll find your actions and movements add to the meaning of the words.

---

**hilding** flibbertigibbet, wild woman
**French slop** baggy trousers
**hams** legs
**pump** shoe

**swits and spurs** urge on your wits, as if you were horse-riding, with whips and spurs
**cheverel** leather that stretches
**ell** forty-five inches

*Enter* ROMEO.

BENVOLIO Here comes Romeo, here comes Romeo.

MERCUTIO Without his roe, like a dried herring: O flesh, flesh, how
art thou fishified! Now is he for the numbers that Petrarch flowed
in. Laura to his lady was a kitchen wench (marry, she had a better      35
love to berhyme her), Dido a dowdy, Cleopatra a gipsy, Helen and
Hero hildings and harlots, Thisbe a grey eye or so, but not to the
purpose. Signior Romeo, 'bon jour'! there's a French salutation
to your French slop. You gave us the counterfeit fairly last night.

ROMEO Good morrow to you both. What counterfeit did I give you?      40

MERCUTIO The slip, sir, the slip, can you not conceive?

ROMEO Pardon, good Mercutio, my business was great, and in such a
case as mine a man may strain courtesy.

MERCUTIO That's as much as to say, such a case as yours constrains
a man to bow in the hams.      45

ROMEO Meaning to cur'sy.

MERCUTIO Thou hast most kindly hit it.

ROMEO A most courteous exposition.

MERCUTIO Nay, I am the very pink of courtesy.

ROMEO Pink for flower.      50

MERCUTIO Right.

ROMEO Why then is my pump well flowered.

MERCUTIO Sure wit! Follow me this jest now, till thou hast worn out
thy pump, that when the single sole of it is worn, the jest may
remain, after the wearing, solely singular.      55

ROMEO O single-soled jest, solely singular for the singleness!

MERCUTIO Come between us, good Benvolio, my wits faints.

ROMEO Swits and spurs, swits and spurs, or I'll cry a match.

MERCUTIO Nay, if our wits run the wild-goose chase, I am done; for
thou hast more of the wild goose in one of thy wits than, I am sure,      60
I have in my whole five. Was I with you there for the goose?

ROMEO Thou wast never with me for any thing when thou wast not
there for the goose.

MERCUTIO I will bite thee by the ear for that jest.

ROMEO Nay, good goose, bite not.      65

MERCUTIO Thy wit is a very bitter sweeting, it is a most sharp sauce.

ROMEO And is it not then well served in to a sweet goose?

MERCUTIO O here's a wit of cheverel, that stretches from an inch
narrow to an ell broad!

*Mercutio's joking becomes more and more sexual. When the Nurse appears, seeking Romeo, Mercutio directs his sexual teasing at her.*

---

### 1 Mercutio's mind

Mercutio relishes his sexual puns. After his fairly conventional use of 'art' four times in lines 73–4 (meaning 'are' or 'skill'), his sexual imagination takes over. Here are just some of his puns: bauble = stick carried by professional fool, *or* penis; hole = hole *or* vagina; tale = story *or* penis. Speak all Mercutio's lines from 72 to 93 as suggestively as you can to bring out his sexual meanings.

Why do you think Shakespeare gave Mercutio this language? If Mercutio were alive today, what job do you think he would be doing?

### 2 'A sail, a sail!' (in pairs)

What is the Nurse wearing to provoke Romeo's cry in line 83? Design a costume that you think fits the Nurse in this scene.

### 3 What's in a name?

Characters' names sometimes contain a clue to their personalities. Mercutio, for example, is like 'mercurial': lively, effervescent, quickly-changing, bouncy. It also is a reminder of Mercury, messenger of the gods, who was a trickster, renowned for eloquence, luck, word-magic and dreams.

Find out all you can about the appropriateness of some of the characters' names, especially Romeo, Escales, Tybalt, Paris, Benvolio, Peter, Sampson. See page 156 for something on the Nurse's name.

---

**broad** indecent ('broad goose' probably means 'dirty-minded')
**natural** idiot
**gear** stuff (joking), or clothes (the Nurse), or sexual organs

**good den** good evening (Elizabethans used this greeting anytime in the afternoon)
**bawd** someone who profits by prostitution. A brothel-keeper
**so ho!** Tallyho!

ROMEO  I stretch it out for that word 'broad', which, added to the goose,   70
proves thee far and wide a broad goose.
MERCUTIO  Why, is not this better now than groaning for love? Now
art thou sociable, now art thou Romeo; now art thou what thou
art, by art as well as by nature, for this drivelling love is like a great
natural that runs lolling up and down to hide his bauble in a hole.   75
BENVOLIO  Stop there, stop there.
MERCUTIO  Thou desirest me to stop in my tale against the hair.
BENVOLIO  Thou wouldst else have made thy tale large.
MERCUTIO  O thou art deceived; I would have made it short, for I was
come to the whole depth of my tale, and meant indeed to occupy   80
the argument no longer.
ROMEO  Here's goodly gear!

*Enter* NURSE *and her man* [PETER].

A sail, a sail!
MERCUTIO  Two, two: a shirt and a smock.
NURSE  Peter!   85
PETER  Anon.
NURSE  My fan, Peter.
MERCUTIO  Good Peter, to hide her face, for her fan's the fairer face.
NURSE  God ye good morrow, gentlemen.
MERCUTIO  God ye good den, fair gentlewoman.   90
NURSE  Is it good den?
MERCUTIO  'Tis no less, I tell ye, for the bawdy hand of the dial is now
upon the prick of noon.
NURSE  Out upon you, what a man are you?
ROMEO  One, gentlewoman, that God hath made, himself to mar.   95
NURSE  By my troth, it is well said: 'for himself to mar', quoth'a?
Gentlemen, can any of you tell me where I may find the young
Romeo?
ROMEO  I can tell you, but young Romeo will be older when you have
found him than he was when you sought him: I am the youngest   100
of that name, for fault of a worse.
NURSE  You say well.
MERCUTIO  Yea, is the worst well? Very well took, i'faith, wisely,
wisely.
NURSE  If you be he, sir, I desire some confidence with you.   105
BENVOLIO  She will indite him to some supper.
MERCUTIO  A bawd, a bawd, a bawd! So ho!

*Mercutio leaves, continuing to mock the Nurse. She protests against his sauciness to her, then cautions Romeo not to deceive Juliet.*

---

## 1 Mercutio's song – something to think about

In lines 111–16, Mercutio is playing his familiar language game, seizing every opportunity for sexual punning. His 'So ho!' (line 107) sets him off on a hunting metaphor: chasing the hare. Here, 'stale', 'hare', 'hoar', can mean or sound like 'whore' – a prostitute. His song has the surface meaning that any old dish is good to eat when you're hungry, but if it goes mouldy, it's not worth paying for ('too much for a score'). Can you work out Mercutio's indecent meaning?

## 2 Mercutio's farewell (in groups of three)

Imagine that the actor playing Mercutio asks you for advice about how he should leave the stage (lines 119–20). Offer him some ideas – and perhaps act out several examples of possible 'business' (stage action) to accompany the words.

## 3 But is it fair? (in groups of four)

Talk together about what you think of the way in which the young men treat the Nurse. Look at how she talks with Romeo from line 136 onwards. Does someone who is so concerned for Juliet's well-being deserve such mocking?

---

**lenten pie** a pie without meat (to be eaten in Lent – when Christians abstained from meat)
**hoars** goes mouldy
**ropery** indecent jokes

**stand to** listen to (but Romeo might also be making a sexual pun)
**flirt-gills** flirts
**skains-mates** cut-throats (though no one really knows what this means)

ROMEO What hast thou found?

MERCUTIO No hare, sir, unless a hare, sir, in a lenten pie, that is
something stale and hoar ere it be spent.                         110

[*He walks by them and sings.*]
An old hare hoar,
And an old hare hoar,
Is very good meat in Lent;
But a hare that is hoar
Is too much for a score,                                          115
When it hoars ere it be spent.
Romeo, will you come to your father's? We'll to dinner thither.

ROMEO I will follow you.

MERCUTIO Farewell, ancient lady, farewell, lady, [*Singing.*] 'lady,
lady'.                                                            120

*Exeunt [Mercutio and Benvolio]*

NURSE I pray you, sir, what saucy merchant was this that was so full
of his ropery?

ROMEO A gentleman, Nurse, that loves to hear himself talk, and will
speak more in a minute than he will stand to in a month.

NURSE And 'a speak any thing against me, I'll take him down, and 'a  125
were lustier than he is, and twenty such Jacks; and if I cannot, I'll
find those that shall. Scurvy knave, I am none of his flirt-gills, I
am none of his skains-mates. [*She turns to Peter, her man.*] And thou
must stand by too and suffer every knave to use me at his pleasure!

PETER I saw no man use you at his pleasure; if I had, my weapon should  130
quickly have been out. I warrant you, I dare draw as soon as another
man, if I see occasion in a good quarrel, and the law on my side.

NURSE Now afore God, I am so vexed that every part about me quivers.
Scurvy knave! Pray you, sir, a word: and as I told you, my young
lady bid me enquire you out; what she bid me say, I will keep to  135
myself. But first let me tell ye, if ye should lead her in a fool's
paradise, as they say, it were a very gross kind of behaviour, as they
say; for the gentlewoman is young; and therefore, if you should deal
double with her, truly it were an ill thing to be offered to any
gentlewoman, and very weak dealing.                               140

ROMEO Nurse, commend me to thy lady and mistress. I protest unto
thee –

NURSE Good heart, and i'faith I will tell her as much. Lord, Lord, she
will be a joyful woman.

*Romeo arranges to marry Juliet that afternoon at Friar Lawrence's cell. He will send a rope ladder to the Nurse so that he may climb to Juliet's room in Capulet's house.*

## 1 Does the Nurse take the money? (in groups of four)

Read lines 151–2 again. Take sides, two for, two against, and argue with reasons.

## 2 'As pale as any clout in the versal world'

The Nurse says Juliet looks as white as a sheet (clout = washed-out rag, versal = 'universal'). But is she telling the truth?

## 3 'R is for the –' (in groups of four)

What was the Nurse about to say in line 175? Talk together about what you think she had in mind when she suddenly stopped. Try to come up with suggestions that you think fit her character. Compare your suggestions with those of other groups.

## 4 Enjoy the Nurse's language (in pairs)

Go back to where the Nurse first speaks in this scene (line 85). Read all her lines aloud, each person reading to a full stop before handing over. Then talk together about what this scene adds to your understanding of the Nurse's character.

**shrift** confession (see page 66)
**shrived** given absolution (pardon) for the sins she has confessed
**tackled stair** rope ladder
**quit** reward

**would fain lay knife aboard** would claim Juliet as his (guests in Elizabethan times brought their own knives to claim a place at table)
**dog-name** 'R' was called the dog's letter because it sounded like a dog growling

ROMEO  What wilt thou tell her, Nurse? thou dost not mark me.                     145
NURSE  I will tell her, sir, that you do protest, which, as I take it, is a
    gentleman-like offer.
ROMEO  Bid her devise
        Some means to come to shrift this afternoon,
        And there she shall at Friar Lawrence' cell                          150
        Be shrived and married. Here is for thy pains.
NURSE  No truly, sir, not a penny.
ROMEO  Go to, I say you shall.
NURSE  This afternoon, sir? Well, she shall be there.
ROMEO  And stay, good Nurse, behind the abbey wall:                             155
        Within this hour my man shall be with thee,
        And bring thee cords made like a tackled stair,
        Which to the high top-gallant of my joy
        Must be my convoy in the secret night.
        Farewell, be trusty, and I'll quit thy pains.                        160
        Farewell, commend me to thy mistress.
NURSE  Now God in heaven bless thee! Hark you, sir.
ROMEO  What say'st thou, my dear Nurse?
NURSE  Is your man secret? Did you ne'er hear say,
        'Two may keep counsel, putting one away'?                            165
ROMEO  'Warrant thee, my man's as true as steel.
NURSE  Well, sir, my mistress is the sweetest lady – Lord, Lord! when
    'twas a little prating thing – O, there is a nobleman in town, one
    Paris, that would fain lay knife aboard; but she, good soul, had as
    lieve see a toad, a very toad, as see him. I anger her sometimes,     170
    and tell her that Paris is the properer man, but I'll warrant you,
    when I say so, she looks as pale as any clout in the versal world.
    Doth not rosemary and Romeo begin both with a letter?
ROMEO  Ay, Nurse, what of that? Both with an R.
NURSE  Ah, mocker, that's the dog-name. R is for the – no, I know it       175
    begins with some other letter – and she hath the prettiest sententious
    of it, of you and rosemary, that it would do you good to hear it.
ROMEO  Commend me to thy lady.
NURSE  Ay, a thousand times.
                                             *[Exit Romeo]*
                  Peter!
PETER  Anon.                                                                     180
NURSE  [*Handing him her fan.*] Before and apace.
                              *Exit [after Peter]*

*Juliet is impatient for the Nurse's return. The Nurse finally arrives, grumbling of her aches and pains.*

---

## 1 What is Juliet's mood? (in pairs)

Read Juliet's lines 1–19 to each other, sharing the lines between you in any manner you wish. Try reading them in three or four different ways, then talk together about Juliet's mood at this moment.

## 2 Feel the movement in Juliet's language (in pairs)

Take Juliet's lines 1–19. From each line, say aloud just one word connected with movement (e.g. line 1, 'send'). How many of these 'movement' words can you find?

## 3 Try writing a couplet

Look at lines 16–7. Make up your own couplet in the same style, beginning 'But old folks . . .'.

## 4 What has the Nurse been doing?

Juliet sent the Nurse at nine o'clock, but she met Romeo at twelve. What's she been doing from nine until twelve?

---

**nimble-pinioned doves** swift-winged doves pulling the chariot of Venus, goddess of love

**bandy** strike to and fro (like a tennis ball)

**jaunce** exhausting, bumpy journey

## ACT 2   SCENE 5
## Capulet's mansion

*Enter* JULIET.

JULIET  The clock struck nine when I did send the Nurse;
　　　In half an hour she promised to return.
　　　Perchance she cannot meet him: that's not so.
　　　O, she is lame! Love's heralds should be thoughts,
　　　Which ten times faster glides than the sun's beams,　5
　　　Driving back shadows over low'ring hills;
　　　Therefore do nimble-pinioned doves draw Love,
　　　And therefore hath the wind-swift Cupid wings.
　　　Now is the sun upon the highmost hill
　　　Of this day's journey, and from nine till twelve　10
　　　Is three long hours, yet she is not come.
　　　Had she affections and warm youthful blood,
　　　She would be as swift in motion as a ball;
　　　My words would bandy her to my sweet love,
　　　And his to me.　15
　　　But old folks, many feign as they were dead,
　　　Unwieldy, slow, heavy, and pale as lead.

*Enter* NURSE [*with* PETER].

　　　O God, she comes! O honey Nurse, what news?
　　　Hast thou met with him? Send thy man away.
NURSE  Peter, stay at the gate.　20
　　　　　　　　　　　　　　　　　[*Exit Peter*]
JULIET  Now, good sweet Nurse – O Lord, why look'st thou sad?
　　　Though news be sad, yet tell them merrily;
　　　If good, thou shamest the music of sweet news
　　　By playing it to me with so sour a face.
NURSE  I am a-weary, give me leave a while.　25
　　　Fie, how my bones ache! What a jaunce have I!
JULIET  I would thou hadst my bones, and I thy news.
　　　Nay, come, I pray thee speak, good, good Nurse, speak.
NURSE  Jesu, what haste! can you not stay a while?
　　　Do you not see that I am out of breath?　30

*Juliet is increasingly frustrated by the Nurse's irrelevant replies. At last, Juliet hears the longed-for news: Romeo waits to marry her at Friar Lawrence's cell.*

## 1 Stage the scene (in pairs)

Read through the whole scene, one person as Juliet, the other as the Nurse. Just enjoy how the Nurse keeps Juliet waiting, until she finally tells the news of Romeo. After reading it, work out how to stage the scene. Write notes for the actors, suggesting how to show the changing moods of Juliet and the Nurse.

Best of all – act it out!

Juliet and the Nurse.
Which line do you think is being spoken at this moment?

**stay the circumstance** wait for the details
**marry come up, I trow** expressions of impatience (by the Virgin Mary, hang on, I trust)
**coil** fuss

JULIET How art thou out of breath, when thou hast breath
To say to me that thou art out of breath?
The excuse that thou dost make in this delay
Is longer than the tale thou dost excuse.
Is thy news good or bad? Answer to that.                    35
Say either, and I'll stay the circumstance:
Let me be satisfied, is't good or bad?
NURSE Well, you have made a simple choice, you know not how to
choose a man: Romeo? no, not he; though his face be better than
any man's, yet his leg excels all men's, and for a hand and a foot    40
and a body, though they be not to be talked on, yet they are past
compare. He is not the flower of courtesy, but I'll warrant him, as
gentle as a lamb. Go thy ways, wench, serve God. What, have you
dined at home?
JULIET No, no! But all this did I know before.                    45
What says he of our marriage, what of that?
NURSE Lord, how my head aches! what a head have I!
It beats as it would fall in twenty pieces.
My back a't'other side – ah, my back, my back!
Beshrew your heart for sending me about                    50
To catch my death with jauncing up and down!
JULIET I'faith, I am sorry that thou art not well.
Sweet, sweet, sweet Nurse, tell me, what says my love?
NURSE Your love says, like an honest gentleman,
And a courteous, and a kind, and a handsome,                    55
And I warrant a virtuous – Where is your mother?
JULIET Where is my mother? why, she is within,
Where should she be? How oddly thou repliest:
'Your love says, like an honest gentleman,
"Where is your mother?"'
NURSE                               O God's lady dear,            60
Are you so hot? Marry come up, I trow;
Is this the poultice for my aching bones?
Henceforward do your messages yourself.
JULIET Here's such a coil! Come, what says Romeo?
NURSE Have you got leave to go to shrift today?                    65
JULIET I have.
NURSE Then hie you hence to Friar Lawrence' cell,
There stays a husband to make you a wife.

*The Nurse, with a sexual joke, sends Juliet off to her marriage with Romeo. In the next scene, Friar Lawrence and Romeo await Juliet. Romeo longs for marriage, but his words have an ominous ring.*

## 1 'Now comes the wanton blood up in your cheeks'

Here's a vivid way of saying 'you're blushing!'. Think of other striking ways of telling someone they are embarrassed.

## 2 Juliet's exit (in groups of four)

Work out how Juliet and the Nurse would leave the stage at the end of this scene. Make sure the way they leave matches their feelings and language.

## 3 Keeping someone waiting . . . an improvisation (in pairs)

Improvise a situation where someone is desperate for news, but the person with that news deliberately delays telling it.

## 4 Love-devouring Death (in groups of six)

Involve everyone in making a tableau entitled 'Love-devouring Death'. Let your imaginations run to produce as dramatic a 'picture' as possible. Compare your group's image with those of other groups, then write a short poem with the title 'Love-devouring Death'.

## 5 Personification – a figure of speech

'Love-devouring Death' is a personification. Death is often turned into a person in the play.

Find two or three other examples of personification. Either draw them or, in a group, prepare tableaux to represent them. Other groups guess which phrase you have chosen.

---

**wanton** uncontrolled
**that after-hours . . . not** so that
  we are not punished with sadness
  later
**countervail** outweigh

Now comes the wanton blood up in your cheeks,
They'll be in scarlet straight at any news. 70
Hie you to church, I must another way,
To fetch a ladder, by the which your love
Must climb a bird's nest soon when it is dark.
I am the drudge, and toil in your delight;
But you shall bear the burden soon at night. 75
Go, I'll to dinner, hie you to the cell.
JULIET  Hie to high fortune! Honest Nurse, farewell.

*Exeunt*


# ACT 2   SCENE 6
## Friar Lawrence's cell

Enter FRIAR LAWRENCE and ROMEO.

FRIAR LAWRENCE  So smile the heavens upon this holy act,
That after-hours with sorrow chide us not.
ROMEO  Amen, amen! but come what sorrow can,
It cannot countervail the exchange of joy
That one short minute gives me in her sight. 5
Do thou but close our hands with holy words,
Then love-devouring Death do what he dare,
It is enough I may but call her mine.

*The Friar advises moderation in love, not violent excess. In reply to Romeo's elaborate language, Juliet speaks of her true love. They leave to be married.*

## 1 Fire and gunpowder – language work (in groups of four)

Read the four short speeches (lines 9–15, 16–20, 24–9, 30–4) to each other several times. Discuss how you feel about them. What seems to be the mood of each?

It will help if you talk about the imagery in each of the speeches. For example, the Friar begins with an image of joyous love as fire and gunpowder which destroy ('consume') at the very moment ('triumph') of meeting ('kiss').

## 2 Can true love be measured?

Romeo, in elaborate language, invites Juliet to tell of their love like a rich description ('blazon') of a coat of arms. But Juliet argues ('Conceit more rich in matter than in words', line 30), that true love doesn't need words. It is so rich, it cannot be measured. What do you think?

Later, in *Antony and Cleopatra*, Shakespeare expressed the same idea: 'There's beggary in the love that can be reckoned'.

## 3 Should the marriage ceremony be shown on stage?
(in pairs)

Shakespeare does not show us the wedding of Romeo and Juliet. Talk together about whether you think the dramatic effect of the play would be increased by adding a wedding scene.

Devise a scene showing the wedding to see how well it 'works'.

---

**powder** gunpowder
**confounds** destroys
**bestride the gossamers** walk on
  threads of a spider's web
**ghostly confessor** spiritual adviser

**blazon** describe or portray
**conceit** imagination
**Till Holy Church . . . one** until
  you are joined in marriage by
  proper religious ceremony

FRIAR LAWRENCE These violent delights have violent ends,
    And in their triumph die like fire and powder,       10
    Which as they kiss consume. The sweetest honey
    Is loathsome in his own deliciousness,
    And in the taste confounds the appetite.
    Therefore love moderately, long love doth so;
    Too swift arrives as tardy as too slow.       15

*Enter* JULIET.

    Here comes the lady. O, so light a foot
    Will ne'er wear out the everlasting flint;
    A lover may bestride the gossamers
    That idles in the wanton summer air,
    And yet not fall, so light is vanity.       20
JULIET Good even to my ghostly confessor.
FRIAR LAWRENCE Romeo shall thank thee, daughter, for us both.
    [*Romeo kisses Juliet.*]
JULIET As much to him, else is his thanks too much.
    [*Juliet returns his kiss.*]
ROMEO Ah, Juliet, if the measure of thy joy
    Be heaped like mine, and that thy skill be more       25
    To blazon it, then sweeten with thy breath
    This neighbour air, and let rich music's tongue
    Unfold the imagined happiness that both
    Receive in either by this dear encounter.
JULIET Conceit, more rich in matter than in words,       30
    Brags of his substance, not of ornament;
    They are but beggars that can count their worth,
    But my true love is grown to such excess
    I cannot sum up sum of half my wealth.
FRIAR LAWRENCE
    Come, come with me, and we will make short work,       35
    For by your leaves, you shall not stay alone
    Till Holy Church incorporate two in one.
                              [*Exeunt*]

# Looking back at Act 2
*Activities for groups or individuals*

## 1 Favourite lines

Look back through the act and choose three or four lines that appeal to you. Learn them by heart and work out a way of presenting them together with the favourite lines of other students.

## 2 Characters as animals

In Scene 2, Juliet talks of Romeo as a captive bird. Take three or four of the other characters and think about what animals or birds they might resemble. Make a drawing of one and write a short note about why you see him or her as your chosen animal or bird. Are there clues in the script to help your imagination?

## 3 The balcony scene – a miscellany of words

There are 189 lines in this famous scene in which Romeo and Juliet declare their love. Take the first twenty lines and select from them what you think are the three most important or powerful words. Then take the next twenty lines (lines 21–40) and do the same. Carry on to the end of the scene, making lines 160–89 your final section. You will have collected twenty-seven words (some might be the same word).

*Either* put the words into two groups: Romeo's or Juliet's. Present a shortened 'balcony scene' using only those words.

*or* whilst one person speaks the twenty-seven words, the others present a group mime to express the words.

*or* write the words in any order to make either a short poem or an 'image cluster' (a diagram that links the words together in some way).

## 4 Burlesque or parody – an improvisation

The balcony scene (2.2) is a favourite of comedians, who 'send it up something rotten'. Try your own improvisation on Shakespeare's setting. A boy in love talks with a young girl at an upstairs window; or a girl, downstairs, talks to a boy who is on an upstairs landing; or . . . make up your own situation!

## 5 Two things to find out

- Malapropisms. The Nurse uses malapropisms. 'Confidence' (2.4.105) is her mistake for 'conference'. Benvolio, replying, uses 'indite' (line 106) for 'invite' (presumably mockingly). Malapropisms are named after Mrs Malaprop, who muddled up her language, in Sheridan's play *The Rivals*. Find out more about her in the library. Shakespeare would have known malapropisms as 'cacozelia'.

- Tragic females. Mercutio speaks of Dido, Cleopatra, Helen, Hero and Thisbe (2.4.36–7). Find out more about them in the library. Write an assignment on how they add to your understanding of *Romeo and Juliet*.

## 6 Shakespeare's language

Glance through Scenes 1–6. Five are written in verse, one in prose. Why do you think Shakespeare changed his style from verse to prose in that particular scene?

Next, read aloud the last word only of each line in Scene 3. Then read the last word only of each line in Scene 2. You'll make some interesting discoveries along the way. Talk together about the reasons for the patterns you find.

## 7 More on Shakespeare's language

Here are two difficult, but very revealing exercises. You'll learn a great deal about Shakespeare's craftsmanship from them. You'll also find they help you with your own writing.

> Single-line sentences. Go through the whole act but only read aloud sentences that occupy one line. Don't read any sentence that is longer than one line.

How much of the sense and feeling of the act comes through from this 'single-line' reading?

> Sentences in single syllables. Now repeat the activity, but this time read aloud only one-line sentences that have only single-syllable words in them. There is only one such line in Scene 1, the final line:

'To seek him here that means not to be found'. The first monosyllabic line in Scene 2 is 'That thou, her maid, art far more fair than she'.

When you have made your list, talk together about how Shakespeare uses these monosyllabic sentences to create feeling and atmosphere. How do they give insight into character?

*Benvolio fears meeting the Capulets, knowing a fight will surely follow.*
*Mercutio laughs at his fears, accusing Benvolio of being a*
*quick-tempered quarreller.*

Mercutio, in Zeffirelli's thirteenth-century setting of the play.

Tybalt, in the Royal Shakespeare Company's twentieth-century setting.

## 1 Quarrelling (in pairs)

Mercutio gives five examples of Benvolio's quarrels (lines 15–25). Read them, then invent five equally fantastic reasons for picking a quarrel. Try miming one or two to other students. Can they guess what each quarrel is about?

**men** in modern productions, usually Balthasar and Abram
**drawer** barman
**doublet** tight jacket (like Mercutio's above)

**fee-simple** legal ownership. Benvolio's statement that if he quarrelled like that, he wouldn't last long, ominously forecasts what will happen to Mercutio shortly

# ACT 3   SCENE 1
## Verona, a public place

*Enter* MERCUTIO *and his* PAGE, BENVOLIO, *and men.*

BENVOLIO I pray thee, good Mercutio, let's retire:
   The day is hot, the Capels are abroad,
   And if we meet we shall not scape a brawl,
   For now, these hot days, is the mad blood stirring.

MERCUTIO Thou art like one of these fellows that, when he enters the   5
   confines of a tavern, claps me his sword upon the table, and says
   'God send me no need of thee!'; and by the operation of the second
   cup draws him on the drawer, when indeed there is no need.

BENVOLIO Am I like such a fellow?

MERCUTIO Come, come, thou art as hot a Jack in thy mood as any in   10
   Italy, and as soon moved to be moody, and as soon moody to be
   moved.

BENVOLIO And what to?

MERCUTIO Nay, and there were two such, we should have none shortly,
   for one would kill the other. Thou? why, thou wilt quarrel with   15
   a man that hath a hair more or a hair less in his beard than thou
   hast; thou wilt quarrel with a man for cracking nuts, having no other
   reason but because thou hast hazel eyes. What eye but such an eye
   would spy out such a quarrel? Thy head is as full of quarrels as
   an egg is full of meat, and yet thy head hath been beaten as addle   20
   as an egg for quarrelling. Thou hast quarrelled with a man for
   coughing in the street, because he hath wakened thy dog that hath
   lain asleep in the sun. Didst thou not fall out with a tailor for
   wearing his new doublet before Easter? with another for tying his
   new shoes with old riband? and yet thou wilt tutor me from   25
   quarrelling?

BENVOLIO And I were so apt to quarrel as thou art, any man should
   buy the fee-simple of my life for an hour and a quarter.

MERCUTIO The fee-simple? O simple!

*Mercutio taunts Tybalt, but Tybalt ignores his insults, because he is seeking Romeo. However, Romeo refuses to accept Tybalt's challenge to fight, and tries to placate him.*

## 1 Picking a quarrel . . . and trying to avoid one
(in groups of four)

Each person takes a part: Benvolio, Mercutio, Tybalt, Romeo. Two are out to pick a fight, two wish to avoid one.

Read through lines 30–65 to gain a feeling of what's happening. Next, each person speaks only the words that are intended to avoid or provoke a quarrel. Change parts and repeat the activity to see if the same words are chosen. Talk together about how the words you chose are intended to start a fight – or avoid it.

## 2 '. . . be satisfied' (in groups of four to eight)

Line 65 is an electric moment in the play. As he is now married to Juliet, Romeo is trying to make peace with Tybalt, who is now his kinsman, even though Tybalt has deeply insulted him. Everyone on stage will react dramatically to Romeo's words.

Prepare a tableau to show everyone at the moment when Romeo says 'be satisfied'. Hold the frozen moment for thirty seconds for other groups to compare with their own versions, and to pick out who's who.

## 3 Man . . . or servant?

In lines 49–52, Tybalt, seeing Romeo, says that this is the man he intends to fight. But Mercutio, always alert to double meanings, pretends that 'man' means 'servant' or 'follower'. He says Romeo will never wear the uniform of Tybalt's servants. Only if Tybalt invites Romeo join him at a duelling place ('go before to field'), will Romeo be Tybalt's 'man'. As you will see on page 95, even on the point of death Mercutio revels in the joy of playing with language.

**Petruchio and others** in modern productions, usually Sampson, Gregory and Peter
**good den** good evening
**minstrels** hired musicians
**'zounds** by Christ's wounds (an oath)
**livery** servants' uniform
**appertaining** appropriate

*Enter* TYBALT, PETRUCHIO, *and others.*

BENVOLIO  By my head, here comes the Capulets.                    30
MERCUTIO  By my heel, I care not.
TYBALT  Follow me close, for I will speak to them.
          Gentlemen, good den, a word with one of you.
MERCUTIO  And but one word with one of us? couple it with something,
          make it a word and a blow.                             35
TYBALT  You shall find me apt enough to that, sir, and you will give
          me occasion.
MERCUTIO  Could you not take some occasion without giving?
TYBALT  Mercutio, thou consortest with Romeo.
MERCUTIO  Consort? what, dost thou make us minstrels? And thou    40
          make minstrels of us, look to hear nothing but discords. Here's my
          fiddlestick, here's that shall make you dance. 'Zounds, consort!
BENVOLIO  We talk here in the public haunt of men:
          Either withdraw unto some private place,
          Or reason coldly of your grievances,                   45
          Or else depart; here all eyes gaze on us.
MERCUTIO  Men's eyes were made to look, and let them gaze;
          I will not budge for no man's pleasure, I.

*Enter* ROMEO.

TYBALT  Well, peace be with you, sir, here comes my man.
MERCUTIO  But I'll be hanged, sir, if he wear your livery.        50
          Marry, go before to field, he'll be your follower;
          Your worship in that sense may call him man.
TYBALT  Romeo, the love I bear thee can afford
          No better term than this: thou art a villain.
ROMEO  Tybalt, the reason that I have to love thee                55
          Doth much excuse the appertaining rage
          To such a greeting. Villain am I none;
          Therefore farewell, I see thou knowest me not.
TYBALT  Boy, this shall not excuse the injuries
          That thou hast done me, therefore turn and draw.        60
ROMEO  I do protest I never injuried thee,
          But love thee better than thou canst devise,
          Till thou shalt know the reason of my love;
          And so, good Capulet, which name I tender
          As dearly as mine own, be satisfied.                   65
MERCUTIO  O calm, dishonourable, vile submission!

*Mercutio, angered by Romeo's refusal to fight, challenges Tybalt. Romeo tries to make peace, but his intervention is fatal for Mercutio, who, mortally wounded, curses Montagues and Capulets alike.*

## 1 Why does Mercutio have to die so early in the play? (in groups of four)

This is the last we see of Mercutio, and the play has not yet reached its half-way point. Talk together about why you think Shakespeare 'kills him off' now, rather than letting him survive.

## 2 Mercutio's language (in pairs)

One person reads all Mercutio's lines on the opposite page, but stops at the end of each sentence. The other comments on each sentence, saying to whom the sentence is probably addressed, and describing Mercutio's tone of voice (e.g. angry, serious, mocking, etc.). Change roles and repeat the exercise to see how far you agree with each other.

## 3 How to play Mercutio's death? (in small groups)

In every production of the play, the director and actors have to decide just how to play lines 82–99. For example, when do Mercutio's friends realise that he isn't merely scratched, but mortally wounded?

Talk together about how you think this part of the scene should be played. It may help if each of you takes a role (e.g. director, Mercutio, Benvolio, Romeo, etc.) to argue what kind of performance you think will have the greatest effect on the audience. Stage your version showing how each person behaves moment to moment.

---

'alla stoccata' rapier thrust
dry-beat thrash without drawing
  blood
pilcher scabbard
passado thrust

sped done for, killed
villain fellow. Elizabethans often
  used 'villain' to address servants. It
  was not a term of abuse (unlike the
  use in lines 54, 56 and 92)

'Alla stoccata' carries it away. [*Draws.*]
Tybalt, you rat-catcher, will you walk?

TYBALT  What wouldst thou have with me?

MERCUTIO  Good King of Cats, nothing but one of your nine lives that                70
I mean to make bold withal, and as you shall use me hereafter,
dry-beat the rest of the eight. Will you pluck your sword out of
his pilcher by the ears? Make haste, lest mine be about your ears
ere it be out.

TYBALT  I am for you. [*Drawing.*]                                                    75

ROMEO  Gentle Mercutio, put thy rapier up.

MERCUTIO  Come, sir, your 'passado'.

[*They fight.*]

ROMEO  Draw, Benvolio, beat down their weapons.
Gentlemen, for shame forbear this outrage!
Tybalt, Mercutio, the Prince expressly hath                                           80
Forbid this bandying in Verona streets.

[*Romeo steps between them.*]

Hold, Tybalt! Good Mercutio!

[*Tybalt under Romeo's arm thrusts Mercutio in.*]

*Away Tybalt [with his followers]*

MERCUTIO                                        I am hurt.
A plague a'both houses! I am sped.
Is he gone and hath nothing?

BENVOLIO                                        What, art thou hurt?

MERCUTIO  Ay, ay, a scratch, a scratch, marry, 'tis enough.                           85
Where is my page? Go, villain, fetch a surgeon.

[*Exit Page*]

ROMEO  Courage, man, the hurt cannot be much.

MERCUTIO  No, 'tis not so deep as a well, nor so wide as a church-door,
but 'tis enough, 'twill serve. Ask for me tomorrow, and you shall
find me a grave man. I am peppered, I warrant, for this world. A                      90
plague a'both your houses! 'Zounds, a dog, a rat, a mouse, a cat,
to scratch a man to death! a braggart, a rogue, a villain, that fights
by the book of arithmetic. Why the dev'l came you between us?
I was hurt under your arm.

ROMEO  I thought all for the best.                                                    95

MERCUTIO  Help me into some house, Benvolio,
Or I shall faint. A plague a'both your houses!
They have made worms' meat of me. I have it,
And soundly too. Your houses!

*Exit [with Benvolio]*

*Romeo, his feelings in turmoil at Mercutio's death, kills Tybalt, then flees.*

## 1 What sort of fighting? (in small groups)

In Zeffirelli's film of *Romeo and Juliet*, Romeo pursues Tybalt and kills him in a savage brawl. Stage-fighting is a very carefully thought-out business. Should the fights be staged as dignified, formal fencing matches, rather like the illustrations on page 70, or as brutal, dirty and painful?

Talk together about how Tybalt's death (lines 121–2) might be staged, and decide on your version. Arrange the movements of the fight, but be very careful. The first rule of all stage-fighting is that no one must be hurt. Try everything out in slow motion first.

## 2 'This day's black fate on moe days doth depend'

Romeo fears that the evil outcomes ('black fate') of today's violence lie in the future ('moe (more) days'). Some people argue that this is the point in the play where the tragedy really begins. You may or may not agree with that, but look at what Benvolio and Romeo say in lines 107–15.

Here, Shakespeare uses the language of **Revenge Tragedy**. This type of play was very popular in the 1590s when he was writing Romeo and Juliet. In Revenge Tragedy, the main character is a 'revenger', and his language is high sounding and portentous.

Should these lines be spoken in a declamatory way, or is it possible to speak them in an ordinary, conversational tone? Try saying them in different styles.

How do you think Romeo says line 127, 'O, I am fortune's fool'?

---

**ally** relative
**respective lenity** respectful
  mildness
**above our heads** on the way to
  heaven

**doom thee death**  sentence you
to death

ROMEO  This gentleman, the Prince's near ally,                    100
          My very friend, hath got this mortal hurt
          In my behalf; my reputation stained
          With Tybalt's slander – Tybalt, that an hour
          Hath been my cousin. O sweet Juliet,
          Thy beauty hath made me effeminate,                     105
          And in my temper softened valour's steel!

                    *Enter Benvolio.*

BENVOLIO  O Romeo, Romeo, brave Mercutio is dead.
            That gallant spirit hath aspired the clouds,
            Which too untimely here did scorn the earth.
ROMEO  This day's black fate on moe days doth depend,             110
          This but begins the woe others must end.

                    *[Enter Tybalt.]*

BENVOLIO  Here comes the furious Tybalt back again.
ROMEO  Again, in triumph, and Mercutio slain?
          Away to heaven, respective lenity,
          And fire-eyed fury be my conduct now!                   115
          Now, Tybalt, take the 'villain' back again
          That late thou gavest me, for Mercutio's soul
          Is but a little way above our heads,
          Staying for thine to keep him company:
          Either thou or I, or both, must go with him.            120
TYBALT  Thou wretched boy, that didst consort him here,
          Shalt with him hence.
ROMEO                           This shall determine that.
                    *They fight; Tybalt falls.*
BENVOLIO  Romeo, away, be gone!
            The citizens are up, and Tybalt slain.
            Stand not amazed, the Prince will doom thee death     125
            If thou art taken. Hence be gone, away!
ROMEO  O, I am fortune's fool.
BENVOLIO                        Why dost thou stay?
                                        *Exit Romeo*

          *Enter Citizens [as OFFICERS of the Watch].*

OFFICER  Which way ran he that killed Mercutio?
           Tybalt, that murderer, which way ran he?

*Lady Capulet demands that Romeo must die. Benvolio tells the story of how Mercutio and Tybalt died.*

## 1 Benvolio's story (in groups of four)

Is Benvolio economical with the truth? Discover whether he gives Prince Escales an accurate and unbiased account of the brawl – or whether he tells it from the point of view of a Montague.

One person reads Benvolio's account (133–66), pausing after every couple of lines. At each pause, the others ask Benvolio questions about his story, for example:

- Why did you say 'unlucky'? (lines 134)
- Why do you remind the Prince that Mercutio was his kinsman? (line 136)
- Why do you call Mercutio 'brave'? (line 136)
- Why do you say Tybalt started the quarrel? Did he? (line 143)
  . . . and so on.

## 2 A sword by any other name . . .? – something to think about

Look at the different way Benvolio describes sword-fighting: 'piercing steel' (line 150); 'deadly point to point' (line 151); 'cold death' (line 153); 'agile arm' (line 157); 'fatal points' (line 157); 'envious thrust' (line 159).

Try to think of other ways of describing sword-fighting. Or you might like to take any everyday activity (e.g. bicycling or writing) and try to make up similarly vivid phrases (**metaphors**) which describe those activities. There's more on metaphors on page 212.

**discover** reveal
**manage** progress
**nice** trivial
**unruly spleen** fiery anger
  (Elizabethans thought anger came
  from the spleen)

**martial** warlike
**retorts** returns
**stout** brave

BENVOLIO There lies that Tybalt.
OFFICER                    Up, sir, go with me; 130
   I charge thee in the Prince's name obey.

*Enter* PRINCE, *old* MONTAGUE, CAPULET, *their* WIVES,
*and all.*

PRINCE Where are the vile beginners of this fray?
BENVOLIO O noble Prince, I can discover all
   The unlucky manage of this fatal brawl;
   There lies the man, slain by young Romeo, 135
   That slew thy kinsman, brave Mercutio.
LADY CAPULET Tybalt, my cousin! O my brother's child!
   O Prince! O husband! O, the blood is spilled
   Of my dear kinsman. Prince, as thou art true,
   For blood of ours, shed blood of Montague. 140
   O cousin, cousin!
PRINCE Benvolio, who began this bloody fray?
BENVOLIO Tybalt, here slain, whom Romeo's hand did slay.
   Romeo, that spoke him fair, bid him bethink
   How nice the quarrel was, and urged withal 145
   Your high displeasure; all this, utterèd
   With gentle breath, calm look, knees humbly bowed,
   Could not take truce with the unruly spleen
   Of Tybalt deaf to peace, but that he tilts
   With piercing steel at bold Mercutio's breast, 150
   Who, all as hot, turns deadly point to point,
   And with a martial scorn, with one hand beats
   Cold death aside, and with the other sends
   It back to Tybalt, whose dexterity
   Retorts it. Romeo he cries aloud, 155
   'Hold, friends! friends, part!' and swifter than his tongue,
   His agile arm beats down their fatal points,
   And 'twixt them rushes; underneath whose arm
   An envious thrust from Tybalt hit the life
   Of stout Mercutio, and then Tybalt fled; 160
   But by and by comes back to Romeo,
   Who had but newly entertained revenge,
   And to't they go like lightning, for, ere I
   Could draw to part them, was stout Tybalt slain;

*Lady Capulet, accusing Benvolio of lying, again demands Romeo's death. But Prince Escales orders that, for killing Tybalt, Romeo will be banished from Verona.*

## 1 Lady Capulet: what's she like? (in groups of four)

Read aloud all that Lady Capulet says in this scene (from line 137). Share out the lines between you and try speaking them in a variety of ways, with accompanying gestures.

Talk together about how Lady Capulet's eleven lines add to your knowledge of her character.

## 2 Report the action!

Imagine you are a reporter for *The Verona Mail* (or make up your own newspaper title). Write an account of the events in this scene.

Royal Shakespeare Company, 1973. Can you identify the characters – and the moment in the scene?

---

**hearts' proceeding** emotional actions (bloody brawling)
**amerce** punish

**purchase out** make amends for, excuse

And as he fell, did Romeo turn and fly.                    165
This is the truth, or let Benvolio die.
LADY CAPULET He is a kinsman to the Montague,
Affection makes him false, he speaks not true:
Some twenty of them fought in this black strife,
And all those twenty could but kill one life.              170
I beg for justice, which thou, Prince, must give:
Romeo slew Tybalt, Romeo must not live.
PRINCE Romeo slew him, he slew Mercutio;
Who now the price of his dear blood doth owe?
MONTAGUE Not Romeo, Prince, he was Mercutio's friend;     175
His fault concludes but what the law should end,
The life of Tybalt.
PRINCE                        And for that offence
Immediately we do exile him hence.
I have an interest in your hearts' proceeding:
My blood for your rude brawls doth lie a-bleeding;         180
But I'll amerce you with so strong a fine
That you shall all repent the loss of mine.
I will be deaf to pleading and excuses,
Nor tears nor prayers shall purchase out abuses:
Therefore use none. Let Romeo hence in haste,             185
Else, when he is found, that hour is his last.
Bear hence this body, and attend our will:
Mercy but murders, pardoning those that kill.

                                        *Exeunt*

*Juliet, unaware of the murderous events of the day, and filled with love for Romeo, longs for the night to come.*

---

### 1 Haste and commands (in groups of four)

Sit closely together. One person quietly reads out the speech. The others echo aloud all words that seem to be commands or concerned with speed or haste, for example 'gallop', 'fiery-footed', 'whip', etc. Try the exercise several times, adding actions. Afterwards, talk together about Juliet's feelings.

### 2 'Such a waggoner . . .' (in groups of six to eight)

In Greek mythology, Phaëton was the son of Phoebus (the sun god). He drove the horses pulling his father's chariot (the sun) so recklessly that Zeus, king of the gods, killed him with a thunderbolt.

In your groups, prepare a tableau to show Phaëton's fate. Make your still picture as vivid and dramatic as possible. Each group shows its tableau. How does this image of Phaëton help your understanding of *Romeo and Juliet*?

### 3 Favourite lines and images (in pairs)

Juliet's thirty-one lines are an epithalamium or wedding song. Pick out the lines or words you most enjoy and talk about them with another pair.

### 4 Embarrassed?

In Victorian times, some readers found Juliet's speech embarrassingly sexual. Which lines and words do you think they objected to?

---

**Phoebus' lodging** the west (where the sun sets)
**that runaways' eyes may**
  **wink** over forty different meanings have been suggested. No one can be certain what it means. What do you think?

**stainless** innocent
**hood my unmanned blood,**
  **bating in my cheeks** an untrained hawk unused to men ('unmanned'), fluttered its wings ('bating'), until it was 'hooded' with a black cap (or 'mantle')
  (see page 60)

# ACT 3    SCENE 2
## Juliet's room in Capulet's mansion

*Enter* JULIET *alone.*

JULIET  Gallop apace, you fiery-footed steeds,
       Towards Phoebus' lodging; such a waggoner
       As Phaëton would whip you to the west,
       And bring in cloudy night immediately.
       Spread thy close curtain, love-performing Night,       5
       That runaways' eyes may wink, and Romeo
       Leap to these arms, untalked of and unseen:
       Lovers can see to do their amorous rites
       By their own beauties, or if love be blind,
       It best agrees with night. Come, civil Night,       10
       Thou sober-suited matron all in black,
       And learn me how to lose a winning match,
       Played for a pair of stainless maidenhoods.
       Hood my unmanned blood, bating in my cheeks,
       With thy black mantle, till strange love grow bold,     15
       Think true love acted simple modesty.
       Come, Night, come, Romeo, come, thou day in night,
       For thou wilt lie upon the wings of night,
       Whiter than new snow upon a raven's back.
       Come, gentle Night, come, loving, black-browed Night,    20
       Give me my Romeo, and when I shall die,
       Take him and cut him out in little stars,
       And he will make the face of heaven so fine
       That all the world will be in love with night,
       And pay no worship to the garish sun.       25
       O, I have bought the mansion of a love,
       But not possessed it, and though I am sold,
       Not yet enjoyed. So tedious is this day
       As is the night before some festival
       To an impatient child that hath new robes       30
       And may not wear them. O, here comes my Nurse,

*Juliet, alarmed by the Nurse's mourning for Tybalt's death, thinks that Romeo has died.*

---

## 1 'I', 'ay' and 'eyes' (in groups of four)

Elizabethans not only enjoyed joking puns (of which Mercutio was a master), but also appreciated punning in tragic situations. In lines 45–52 Juliet and the Nurse make much of one vowel sound: 'I'.

Read the lines aloud to each other, in any manner you think appropriate. Then imagine you are directing the play. Work out what advice you would give your two actors as to how they could deliver these eight lines to have the greatest effect on an audience.

## 2 'Vile earth, to earth resign, end motion here' (in pairs)

Juliet wishes that her body ('vile earth') be buried ('to earth resign'), ending her life ('end motion here').

Catch the mood of this part of the scene by reading to your partner just one word from each line (from line 36 onwards) that emphasises death or disaster. Talk together about how your chosen words create a mood for the scene.

## 3 Why does the Nurse mislead Juliet?

Why doesn't the Nurse immediately tell Juliet that it's Tybalt, not Romeo who is dead?

---

**cords** rope ladder
**weraday** alas!
**envious** spiteful
**cockatrice** the basilisk, a legendary beast. Half snake, half cockerel, its stare could kill

**weal** welfare, joy
**corse** corpse
**sounded** swooned
**bankrout** bankrupt (Juliet has lost her 'investment of love' in Romeo)

*Enter* NURSE, *with [the ladder of] cords [in her lap].*

And she brings news, and every tongue that speaks
But Romeo's name speaks heavenly eloquence.
Now, Nurse, what news? What hast thou there? the cords
That Romeo bid thee fetch?

NURSE                                      Ay, ay, the cords.                    35
                    [*Throws them down.*]

JULIET Ay me, what news? Why dost thou wring thy hands?
NURSE Ah weraday, he's dead, he's dead, he's dead!
      We are undone, lady, we are undone.
      Alack the day, he's gone, he's killed, he's dead!
JULIET Can heaven be so envious?
NURSE                                  Romeo can,                              40
      Though heaven cannot. O Romeo, Romeo!
      Who ever would have thought it? Romeo!
JULIET What devil art thou that dost torment me thus?
      This torture should be roared in dismal hell.
      Hath Romeo slain himself? Say thou but 'ay',             45
      And that bare vowel 'I' shall poison more
      Than the death-darting eye of cockatrice.
      I am not I, if there be such an 'ay',
      Or those eyes shut, that makes thee answer 'ay'.
      If he be slain, say 'ay', or if not, 'no':                50
      Brief sounds determine my weal or woe.
NURSE I saw the wound, I saw it with mine eyes
      (God save the mark!), here on his manly breast:
      A piteous corse, a bloody piteous corse,
      Pale, pale as ashes, all bedaubed in blood,              55
      All in gore blood; I sounded at the sight.
JULIET O break, my heart, poor bankrout, break at once!
      To prison, eyes, ne'er look on liberty!
      Vile earth, to earth resign, end motion here,
      And thou and Romeo press one heavy bier!                 60
NURSE O Tybalt, Tybalt, the best friend I had!
      O courteous Tybalt, honest gentleman,
      That ever I should live to see thee dead!
JULIET What storm is this that blows so contrary?
      Is Romeo slaughtered? and is Tybalt dead?               65
      My dearest cousin, and my dearer lord?

*Juliet learns that Tybalt is dead and Romeo banished. She begins to accuse Romeo of seeming beautiful but acting vilely, but then rebukes the Nurse for wishing shame on Romeo.*

## 1  Appearance and reality (in groups of four)

Juliet, hearing of Romeo's killing of Tybalt, laments that a beautiful appearance can hide an evil reality ('beautiful tyrant', 'damned saint' etc.). These 'opposites' are called oxymorons. Romeo has used them earlier (see pages 14 and 212).

How many oxymorons can you count in lines 73–84? Choose one of them and prepare a tableau involving every member of the group. Each group shows its tableau. The other groups guess which oxymorons are portrayed.

## 2  The Nurse's view of men (in pairs)

Look at the seven things the Nurse says about men in lines 85–7. Talk together about why she sets out such a list. Is it because of what she's experienced in the play? Or could there be other reasons? You'll find it helpful to talk about each characteristic in turn ('no trust', 'no faith', etc.).

---

**the general doom** doomsday, the end of the world (sounded by the last trumpet)
**bower** enclose

**perjured** liars
**forsworn** promise breakers
**naught** wicked, vicious
**aqua-vitae** brandy

Then, dreadful trumpet, sound the general doom,
For who is living, if those two are gone?

NURSE  Tybalt is gone and Romeo banishèd,
    Romeo that killed him, he is banishèd.            70

JULIET  O God, did Romeo's hand shed Tybalt's blood?

NURSE  It did, it did, alas the day, it did!

JULIET  O serpent heart, hid with a flow'ring face!
    Did ever dragon keep so fair a cave?
    Beautiful tyrant, fiend angelical!            75
    Dove-feathered raven, wolvish-ravening lamb!
    Despisèd substance of divinest show!
    Just opposite to what thou justly seem'st,
    A damnèd saint, an honourable villain!
    O nature, what hadst thou to do in hell       80
    When thou didst bower the spirit of a fiend
    In mortal paradise of such sweet flesh?
    Was ever book containing such vile matter
    So fairly bound? O that deceit should dwell
    In such a gorgeous palace!

NURSE                    There's no trust,     85
    No faith, no honesty in men, all perjured,
    All forsworn, all naught, all dissemblers.
    Ah, where's my man? Give me some aqua-vitae;
    These griefs, these woes, these sorrows make me old.
    Shame come to Romeo!

JULIET                 Blistered be thy tongue    90
    For such a wish! he was not born to shame:
    Upon his brow shame is ashamed to sit;
    For 'tis a throne where honour may be crowned
    Sole monarch of the universal earth.
    O what a beast was I to chide at him!     95

NURSE  Will you speak well of him that killed your cousin?

JULIET  Shall I speak ill of him that is my husband?
    Ah, poor my lord, what tongue shall smooth thy name,
    When I, thy three-hours wife, have mangled it?
    But wherefore, villain, didst thou kill my cousin?    100
    That villain cousin would have killed my husband.
    Back, foolish tears, back to your native spring,
    Your tributary drops belong to woe,
    Which you mistaking offer up to joy.

*Juliet is devastated by the thought of Romeo's banishment. She threatens to kill herself. But she is cheered by the Nurse's promise to find Romeo and send him to her bedchamber that night.*

## 1 Juliet's moods (in groups of three)

In this scene, Juliet's feelings swing rapidly. Read through all she says from line 1 to line 143. Work out a way of showing her changing moods. It might be a graph, or a series of words, or a sequence of pictures, or a mime that you devise, or . . .

Share and compare your findings with one or two other groups.

## 2 Death and woe (in pairs)

One person quietly reads out every line on the facing page. The other person echoes all words to do with death, woe or suffering. Change roles and repeat the exercise. Then talk together about how such words create the prevailing atmosphere. Where does that gloomy mood change?

## 3 How does Nurse speak line 138?

Find five quite different ways of speaking 'Hie to your chamber'. Which do you prefer?

**fain** gladly
**modern** ordinary
**rear-ward** final word

**beguiled** deceived, cheated
**hie** go at once
**wot well** know well

My husband lives that Tybalt would have slain,                           105
And Tybalt's dead that would have slain my husband:
All this is comfort, wherefore weep I then?
Some word there was, worser than Tybalt's death,
That murdered me; I would forget it fain,
But O, it presses to my memory,                                          110
Like damnèd guilty deeds to sinners' minds:
'Tybalt is dead, and Romeo banishèd.'
That 'banishèd', that one word 'banishèd',
Hath slain ten thousand Tybalts. Tybalt's death
Was woe enough if it had ended there;                                    115
Or if sour woe delights in fellowship,
And needly will be ranked with other griefs,
Why followed not, when she said 'Tybalt's dead',
'Thy father' or 'thy mother', nay, or both,
Which modern lamentation might have moved?                               120
But with a rear-ward following Tybalt's death,
'Romeo is banishèd': to speak that word,
Is father, mother, Tybalt, Romeo, Juliet,
All slain, all dead. 'Romeo is banishèd!'
There is no end, no limit, measure, bound,                               125
In that word's death, no words can that woe sound.
Where is my father and my mother, Nurse?
NURSE Weeping and wailing over Tybalt's corse.
   Will you go to them? I will bring you thither.
JULIET Wash they his wounds with tears? mine shall be spent,            130
   When theirs are dry, for Romeo's banishment.
   Take up those cords. Poor ropes, you are beguiled,
   Both you and I, for Romeo is exiled.
   He made you for a highway to my bed,
   But I, a maid, die maiden-widowèd.                                    135
   Come, cords, come, Nurse, I'll to my wedding bed,
   And death, not Romeo, take my maidenhead!
NURSE Hie to your chamber. I'll find Romeo
   To comfort you, I wot well where he is.
   Hark ye, your Romeo will be here at night.                           140
   I'll to him, he is hid at Lawrence' cell.
JULIET O find him! Give this ring to my true knight,
   And bid him come to take his last farewell.
                                                   *Exeunt*

*Friar Lawrence tells Romeo of the Prince's sentence: he is to be banished from Verona. The news appals Romeo.*

---

## 1 Romeo's entrance (in pairs)

The Friar calls Romeo on stage. Look at the Elizabethan stage on page 214 and suggest how his entrance might be made there. Explore other ways of getting Romeo on stage in other, non-Elizabethan, settings. Remember that he is in hiding, having fled after killing Tybalt.

A modern Romeo and Juliet? Seretse Khama married Ruth Williams. Her father rejected her. The British Government sent Seretse into exile for five years because of the marriage. But the story of Seretse and Ruth ended happily, unlike the play.

---

**fearful** for Elizabethans, 'fearful' meant both 'full of fear' and 'terrible' or 'fatal'. Do you think Romeo is a frightening or fatal character?

**enamoured of thy parts** in love with

**doom** sentence

**sour company** sorrow

**without** outside

**purgatory** where the dead suffered torment

**mistermed** wrongly named

## ACT 3   SCENE 3
## Friar Lawrence's cell

Enter FRIAR LAWRENCE.

FRIAR LAWRENCE
    Romeo, come forth, come forth, thou fearful man:
    Affliction is enamoured of thy parts,
    And thou art wedded to calamity.

[*Enter*] ROMEO.

ROMEO Father, what news? What is the Prince's doom?
    What sorrow craves acquaintance at my hand,     5
    That I yet know not?
FRIAR LAWRENCE           Too familiar
    Is my dear son with such sour company!
    I bring thee tidings of the Prince's doom.
ROMEO What less than doomsday is the Prince's doom?
FRIAR LAWRENCE A gentler judgement vanished from his lips:     10
    Not body's death, but body's banishment.
ROMEO Ha, banishment? be merciful, say 'death':
    For exile hath more terror in his look,
    Much more than death. Do not say 'banishment'!
FRIAR LAWRENCE Here from Verona art thou banishèd.     15
    Be patient, for the world is broad and wide.
ROMEO There is no world without Verona walls,
    But purgatory, torture, hell itself:
    Hence 'banishèd' is banished from the world,
    And world's exile is death; then 'banishèd'     20
    Is death mistermed. Calling death 'banishèd',
    Thou cut'st my head off with a golden axe,
    And smilest upon the stroke that murders me.

*Romeo, distraught because banishment will mean he can no longer be with Juliet, refuses to be comforted by Friar Lawrence.*

---

## 1 Separated lovers (in groups of four or five)

Here's an exercise that is challenging but rewarding. Take Romeo's lines 29–51 opposite and Juliet's lines 97–126 in the preceding scene (pages 107–09). Explore how they reflect or contrast with each other. You could try 'intercutting' them, taking a line or two of Juliet's, followed by a line of Romeo's and so on. Be adventurous! Don't be afraid to play with the sequence of the lines. Make up a dramatic presentation entitled 'Banishment'. It should show the two young lovers, separated, facing a bleak future, but united in their desolation and grief.

## 2 'Adversity's sweet milk, philosophy' – arrange a debate

Friar Lawrence argues that philosophy (thinking, reasoning) will comfort someone in adversity (beset by problems). Romeo angrily dismisses that advice ('Hang up philosophy!') because thinking without action is no help.

Do you favour the Friar's argument or Romeo's? Take sides and argue your case – either using Romeo's situation, or taking examples from your own experience.

## 3 Death or banishment? (in groups of four)

Romeo finds the thought of banishment far worse than death. Many people today find that unbelievable.

What do you think? Work out a modern situation in which you will never again be allowed to see the person you most love. Then argue whether you think that is the worst thing that could possibly happen.

---

**validity** value
**courtship** courtly behaviour
  (or 'wooing')
**vestal** virginal
**ghostly confessor** spiritual adviser

**sin-absolver** someone who
  forgives sins
**fond** foolish
**displant** uproot
**doom** death sentence

FRIAR LAWRENCE O deadly sin! O rude unthankfulness!
    Thy fault our law calls death, but the kind Prince,      25
    Taking thy part, hath rushed aside the law,
    And turned that black word 'death' to 'banishment'.
    This is dear mercy, and thou seest it not.
ROMEO 'Tis torture, and not mercy. Heaven is here
    Where Juliet lives, and every cat and dog      30
    And little mouse, every unworthy thing,
    Live here in heaven, and may look on her,
    But Romeo may not. More validity,
    More honourable state, more courtship lives
    In carrion flies than Romeo; they may seize      35
    On the white wonder of dear Juliet's hand,
    And steal immortal blessing from her lips,
    Who even in pure and vestal modesty
    Still blush, as thinking their own kisses sin;
    But Romeo may not, he is banishèd.      40
    Flies may do this, but I from this must fly;
    They are free men, but I am banishèd:
    And sayest thou yet that exile is not death?
    Hadst thou no poison mixed, no sharp-ground knife,
    No sudden mean of death, though ne'er so mean,      45
    But 'banishèd' to kill me? 'Banishèd'?
    O Friar, the damnèd use that word in hell;
    Howling attends it. How hast thou the heart,
    Being a divine, a ghostly confessor,
    A sin-absolver, and my friend professed,      50
    To mangle me with that word 'banishèd'?
FRIAR LAWRENCE Thou fond mad man, hear me a little speak.
ROMEO O thou wilt speak again of banishment.
FRIAR LAWRENCE I'll give thee armour to keep off that word:
    Adversity's sweet milk, philosophy,      55
    To comfort thee though thou art banishèd.
ROMEO Yet 'banishèd'? Hang up philosophy!
    Unless philosophy can make a Juliet,
    Displant a town, reverse a prince's doom,
    It helps not, it prevails not; talk no more.      60
FRIAR LAWRENCE O then I see that mad men have no ears.
ROMEO How should they when that wise men have no eyes?

*Romeo, bewailing all that's happened, falls weeping to the ground and ignores the Friar's pleas to stand up. The Nurse arrives and also begs him to stand.*

## 1 Acting the words (in pairs)

One person reads Romeo's lines 64–70. The other accompanies them with gestures. Change roles and repeat the exercise. Talk together about how Shakespeare builds his stage directions into his language. What advice would you give to an actor on how to deliver these seven lines?

## 2 More staging (in pairs)

Friar Lawrence's lines 74–80 show his agitation. Work together as in 'Acting the words' above. First, try out some actions as your partner reads. Then work out what advice you would give the actor playing Friar Lawrence.

## 3 Can adults understand? (in groups of four)

Romeo accuses the Friar of not being able to understand how a young person feels (lines 64–70).

Do you agree with him? Take roles and improvise a situation where an older person wishes to give advice to someone of your age.

## 4 The Nurse – or Shakespeare's writing

Some people feel uncomfortable because even at this serious moment the Nurse uses words with sexual double meanings ('case', 'stand', 'rise', or 'O'). Why do you think the Nurse uses such language? Does it add to or detract from the dramatic impact?

---

**estate** situation
**doting** loving madly

**case** condition
**so deep an O** such moaning

FRIAR LAWRENCE Let me dispute with thee of thy estate.

ROMEO Thou canst not speak of that thou dost not feel.

    Wert thou as young as I, Juliet thy love,        65
    An hour but married, Tybalt murderèd,
    Doting like me, and like me banishèd,
    Then mightst thou speak, then mightst thou tear thy hair,
    And fall upon the ground as I do now,
    Taking the measure of an unmade grave.        70

        *Enter Nurse [within] and knock.*

FRIAR LAWRENCE Arise, one knocks. Good Romeo, hide thyself.

ROMEO Not I, unless the breath of heart-sick groans
    Mist-like infold me from the search of eyes.
           *Knock.*

FRIAR LAWRENCE
    Hark how they knock! – Who's there? – Romeo, arise,
    Thou wilt be taken. – Stay a while! – Stand up;     75
        *Loud knock.*
    Run to my study. – By and by! – God's will,
    What simpleness is this? – I come, I come!
          *Knock.*
    Who knocks so hard? whence come you? what's your will?

NURSE [*Within*] Let me come in, and you shall know my errand:
    I come from Lady Juliet.

FRIAR LAWRENCE           Welcome then. [*Unlocks the door.*]   80

        *Enter NURSE.*

NURSE O holy Friar, O tell me, holy Friar,
    Where's my lady's lord? where's Romeo?

FRIAR LAWRENCE
    There on the ground, with his own tears made drunk.

NURSE O he is even in my mistress' case,
    Just in her case. O woeful sympathy!        85
    Piteous predicament! even so lies she,
    Blubb'ring and weeping, weeping and blubb'ring.
    Stand up, stand up, stand, and you be a man;
    For Juliet's sake, for her sake, rise and stand;
    Why should you fall into so deep an O?       90

*On hearing the Nurse tell of Juliet's sorrow, Romeo tries to stab himself. The Nurse seizes his dagger and Friar Lawrence rebukes him for his suicide attempt.*

## 1 Who snatches the dagger? (in groups of three)

Some people believe that Shakespeare did not include this stage direction (line 108), but that the actor playing the Nurse added it. Act out different versions of lines 105–11. What difference does it make if the Friar, rather than the Nurse, snatches the dagger away from Romeo? ('sack the hateful mansion' means 'destroy my body'.)

## 2 The Friar rebukes Romeo (in groups of six)

Read the Friar's lines 108–34. Each person reads only to a punctuation mark before handing on to the next reader. Talk together about the Friar's view of the relations of men, women and beasts. Then take it a line at a time. Speak only one word from each line – the word you think will have most effect on Romeo. Try this several times. Are the same words chosen each time?

## 3 What's in a name? (lines 102–7)

Look back to Act 2, Scene 2, lines 38–57, where Juliet talks of names. Explore the relationships of the speeches.

## 4 'Thou sham'st thy shape, thy love, thy wit'

The Friar says Romeo shames his good looks ('shape') his declarations of love ('love') and his intelligence ('wit'). He's like a stingy money-lender ('usurer') because, although he possesses those excellent qualitites in abundance he doesn't use them properly. Read what the Friar says about each quality (lines 126–34). Can you imagine a picture for each one?

**concealed lady** secret wife
**rail'st** complain
**usurer** money-lender
**bedeck** decorate

**form of wax** waxwork, easily melted
**digressing** deviating, or taking away from

ROMEO  Nurse! [*He rises.*]

NURSE  Ah, sir, ah, sir, death's the end of all.

ROMEO  Spakest thou of Juliet? how is it with her?
      Doth not she think me an old murderer,
      Now I have stained the childhood of our joy          95
      With blood removed but little from her own?
      Where is she? and how doth she? and what says
      My concealed lady to our cancelled love?

NURSE  O she says nothing, sir, but weeps and weeps,
      And now falls on her bed, and then starts up,      100
      And Tybalt calls, and then on Romeo cries,
      And then down falls again.

ROMEO                      As if that name,
      Shot from the deadly level of a gun,
      Did murder her, as that name's cursèd hand
      Murdered her kinsman. O tell me, Friar, tell me,      105
      In what vile part of this anatomy
      Doth my name lodge? Tell me, that I may sack
      The hateful mansion.

[*He offers to stab himself, and Nurse snatches the dagger away.*]

FRIAR LAWRENCE              Hold thy desperate hand!
      Art thou a man? thy form cries out thou art;
      Thy tears are womanish, thy wild acts denote      110
      The unreasonable fury of a beast.
      Unseemly woman in a seeming man,
      And ill-beseeming beast in seeming both,
      Thou hast amazed me. By my holy order,
      I thought thy disposition better tempered.      115
      Hast thou slain Tybalt? wilt thou slay thyself,
      And slay thy lady that in thy life lives,
      By doing damnèd hate upon thyself?
      Why rail'st thou on thy birth? the heaven and earth?
      Since birth, and heaven, and earth, all three do meet      120
      In thee at once, which thou at once wouldst lose.
      Fie, fie, thou sham'st thy shape, thy love, thy wit,
      Which like a usurer abound'st in all,
      And usest none in that true use indeed
      Which should bedeck thy shape, thy love, thy wit:      125
      Thy noble shape is but a form of wax,
      Digressing from the valour of a man;

Romeo and Juliet

*Friar Lawrence rebukes Romeo for his lack of manliness, love and intelligence. He reminds Romeo of his good fortune and plans how he can eventually be recalled from exile.*

## 1 The Friar's speech – keeping audience interest
(in groups of three)

The Friar delivers his long speech (lines 108–58), first rebuking Romeo, then seeking to cheer him, then setting out a plan of action. Imagine you are directing the play. Work out how you would keep the audience constantly interested. Offer advice to the three actors (the Friar, Romeo, the Nurse) how they should behave and move throughout the speech. It will help if each of you takes a role, working out your solution practically as you go through the speech.

## 2 Everyone joins in! (a whole class exercise)

You can do this seated at your desks. One person reads the Friar's speech (lines 108–58) aloud, pausing frequently. Everyone else mimes appropriate expressions and movements for each section of the speech. Use only hands, faces and arms. Freeze occasionally for everyone to compare. You'll not only find it fun, but fascinating to see the different ways of representing the same line or image!

## 3 Act out the Friar's plan (in groups of five or six)

The Friar sets out his plan in lines 146–57. Act out the lines as the Friar imagines the action. Try to show every action he describes. It's quite a story!

---

**perjury** oath-breaking, false promising
**flask** a container for gunpowder
**mishaved** misbehaved

**Watch be set** police come on duty (see note about the Watch on page 182)
**blaze** announce

Thy dear love sworn but hollow perjury,
Killing that love which thou hast vowed to cherish;
Thy wit, that ornament to shape and love,                            130
Misshapen in the conduct of them both,
Like powder in a skilless soldier's flask,
Is set afire by thine own ignorance,
And thou dismembered with thine own defence.
What, rouse thee, man! thy Juliet is alive,                          135
For whose dear sake thou wast but lately dead:
There art thou happy. Tybalt would kill thee,
But thou slewest Tybalt: there art thou happy.
The law that threatened death becomes thy friend,
And turns it to exile: there art thou happy.                         140
A pack of blessings light upon thy back,
Happiness courts thee in her best array,
But like a mishavèd and sullen wench,
Thou pouts upon thy fortune and thy love:
Take heed, take heed, for such die miserable.                        145
Go get thee to thy love as was decreed,
Ascend her chamber, hence and comfort her;
But look thou stay not till the Watch be set,
For then thou canst not pass to Mantua,
Where thou shalt live till we can find a time                        150
To blaze your marriage, reconcile your friends,
Beg pardon of the Prince, and call thee back
With twenty hundred thousand times more joy
Than thou went'st forth in lamentation.
Go before, Nurse, commend me to thy lady,                            155
And bid her hasten all the house to bed,
Which heavy sorrow makes them apt unto.
Romeo is coming.
NURSE O Lord, I could have stayed here all the night
        To hear good counsel. O, what learning is!                   160
        My lord, I'll tell my lady you will come.
ROMEO Do so, and bid my sweet prepare to chide.
            [*Nurse offers to go in, and turns again.*]
NURSE Here, sir, a ring she bid me give you, sir.
        Hie you, make haste, for it grows very late.
ROMEO How well my comfort is revived by this.                        165
                                            [*Exit Nurse*]

119

*Friar Lawrence sends Romeo to Juliet, warning him to leave early for
Mantua and await news. In Scene 4, Capulet tells Paris that because of
Tybalt's death, he has not yet talked with Juliet about marriage.*

## 1 Romeo's changing emotions (in pairs)

Look back through Scene 3 and trace the swings of Romeo's moods.
Some people think his emotions are too extreme and that he really
doesn't think about Juliet at all, only his own misery.

Talk together about where you think Romeo's feelings and
language are genuine and where you think they are 'over the top'.
Work out a way of representing the changes in Romeo's moods
through the scene, using a diagram, a graph, or a cartoon sequence,
etc.

## 2 Fathers and daughters – something to find out

Capulet is certain that Juliet will obey him ('I think she will be ruled in
all respects by me; nay more, I doubt it not'). Shakespeare often wrote
about fathers who wished to dominate their daughters' lives. Here are
some of the daughters' names: Cordelia, Hero, Imogen, Desdemona,
Portia, Ophelia, Miranda, Celia, Hermia. Can you identify the plays
in which they appear?

## 3 Focus on Paris (in groups of four)

Talk together about your views of Paris. How old is he? What does he
look like? Then concentrate on how you think he should behave in
this short scene. Work out your advice to the actor playing Paris on
movements, gestures and speech.

---

**here stands all your state** here is
  your future
**sojourn** stay, wait
**hap** happening

**mewed up to her heaviness** caged
  up in her sorrow (falcons were kept
  caged in mews)
**desperate tender** bold offer

FRIAR LAWRENCE
> Go hence, good night, and here stands all your state:
> Either be gone before the Watch be set,
> Or by the break of day disguised from hence.
> Sojourn in Mantua; I'll find out your man,
> And he shall signify from time to time                    170
> Every good hap to you that chances here.
> Give me thy hand, 'tis late. Farewell, good night.

ROMEO  But that a joy past joy calls out on me,
> It were a grief, so brief to part with thee:
> Farewell.                                                 175

*Exeunt*


# ACT 3   SCENE 4
## Capulet's mansion

*Enter old* CAPULET, *his* WIFE, *and* PARIS.

CAPULET  Things have fall'n out, sir, so unluckily
> That we have had no time to move our daughter.
> Look you, she loved her kinsman Tybalt dearly,
> And so did I. Well, we were born to die.
> 'Tis very late, she'll not come down tonight.             5
> I promise you, but for your company,
> I would have been abed an hour ago.

PARIS  These times of woe afford no times to woo.
> Madam, good night, commend me to your daughter.

LADY CAPULET  I will, and know her mind early tomorrow;     10
> Tonight she's mewed up to her heaviness.
> [*Paris offers to go in, and Capulet calls him again.*]

CAPULET  Sir Paris, I will make a desperate tender
> Of my child's love: I think she will be ruled
> In all respects by me; nay more, I doubt it not.

*Capulet instructs his wife to tell Juliet that she is to be married to Paris. He decides the wedding will be in three days' time.*

---

## 1 What does Lady Capulet think of her husband?
(in groups of three)

Every production of the play has to address the question of how Juliet's parents feel about each other. Do they love each other? Did they love each other when they married?

Act out the whole scene, but with Lady Capulet commenting on everything her husband says. Try it in a number of ways: does she find him tiresome and boring? or is she afraid of him? or is she still in love with him? Did she have a father like her husband? (see 1.3.73). Can you agree on which you prefer?

And what does Capulet think of his wife?

## 2 Time begins to run faster (in pairs)

Read through this scene aloud emphasising all the words to do with time. How many can you count? Notice how this adds to the sense of fast-moving events.

Then read Capulet's lines 19–35, but in a jerky, hasty manner. Talk about whether this way of reading catches the gathering momentum of events.

## 3 Dramatic irony (in pairs)

Capulet's last two lines (lines 34–5) are an example of **dramatic irony** (when the audience knows something the character does not know). Talk together about why the lines contain dramatic irony.

---

**my son** Capulet already sees Paris
 as his son-in-law
**by and by** soon
**afore me** indeed

Wife, go you to her ere you go to bed,                                    15
Acquaint her here of my son Paris' love,
And bid her – mark you me? – on Wednesday next –
But soft, what day is this?
PARIS                                      Monday, my lord.
CAPULET  Monday, ha, ha! Well, Wednesday is too soon,
A'Thursday let it be – a'Thursday, tell her,                              20
She shall be married to this noble earl.
Will you be ready? do you like this haste?
Well, keep no great ado – a friend or two,
For hark you, Tybalt being slain so late,
It may be thought we held him carelessly,                                25
Being our kinsman, if we revel much:
Therefore we'll have some half a dozen friends,
And there an end. But what say you to Thursday?
PARIS  My lord, I would that Thursday were tomorrow.
CAPULET  Well, get you gone, a'Thursday be it then. –                     30
Go you to Juliet ere you go to bed,
Prepare her, wife, against this wedding day.
Farewell, my lord. Light to my chamber, ho!
Afore me, it is so very late that we
May call it early by and by. Good night.                                 35

                                                            *Exeunt*

*After their wedding night together, Juliet tries to persuade Romeo that it is not yet dawn, not yet time for him to leave her.*

## 1 Stage the opening (in groups of four)

Talk together about possible ways of staging the opening of this scene. How would it work on the Elizabethan stage (see page 214)?

## 2 How should the lines be spoken? (in pairs)

Try different ways of speaking lines 1–25 (e.g. Juliet as loving, or impatient, or bossy or sleepy, or . . .). Romeo as loving, or afraid, or secretly desiring to go, or irritable . . .). Can you agree on how you think the lines should be delivered? In particular, how should lines 11 and 12 be spoken? Pick one or two favourite lines. Talk with other students about why you enjoy 'your' lines.

## 3 What would happen? (in groups of three)

Imagine Lady Capulet bursts in just as Romeo speaks line 11. Improvise what would happen.

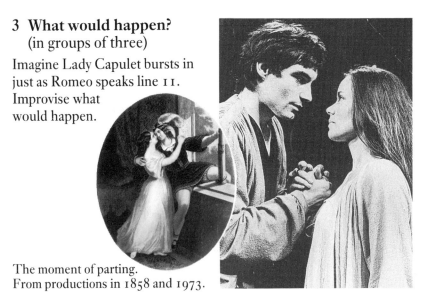

The moment of parting.
From productions in 1858 and 1973.

---

**jocund** cheerful
**some meteor that the sun exhaled** meteors were thought to be caused by the sun drawing up vapours from the earth and igniting them

**tane** captured (taken)
**reflex of Cynthia's brow** reflection of the edge of the moon (Cynthia is the moon goddess)

# ACT 3  SCENE 5
## Juliet's bedroom

*Enter* ROMEO *and* JULIET *aloft at the window.*

JULIET  Wilt thou be gone? It is not yet near day:
It was the nightingale, and not the lark,
That pierced the fearful hollow of thine ear;
Nightly she sings on yond pomegranate tree.
Believe me, love, it was the nightingale.                    5

ROMEO  It was the lark, the herald of the morn,
No nightingale. Look, love, what envious streaks
Do lace the severing clouds in yonder east:
Night's candles are burnt out, and jocund day
Stands tiptoe on the misty mountain tops.                    10
I must be gone and live, or stay and die.

JULIET  Yond light is not daylight, I know it, I:
It is some meteor that the sun exhaled
To be to thee this night a torch-bearer,
And light thee on thy way to Mantua.                         15
Therefore stay yet, thou need'st not to be gone.

ROMEO  Let me be tane, let me be put to death,
I am content, so thou wilt have it so.
I'll say yon grey is not the morning's eye,
'Tis but the pale reflex of Cynthia's brow;                  20
Nor that is not the lark whose notes do beat
The vaulty heaven so high above our heads.
I have more care to stay than will to go:
Come, death, and welcome! Juliet wills it so.
How is't, my soul? Let's talk, it is not day.                25

Apsorry

*Juliet accepts that it is morning and time to part. The Nurse warns the lovers that Lady Capulet is coming. As Romeo leaves, Juliet's words are filled with foreboding.*

### 1 'Some say the lark and loathèd toad changed eyes'

There was a belief that skylarks and toads had exchanged eyes. This explained why toads' eyes were thought to be more beautiful than larks' eyes. Juliet wishes they had exchanged voices too, because the harsh voice of the toad is more suitable to the lovers' sad parting. If you were making a film of the play, and were asked to 'dub in' or add a sad or ominous sound as background here, what sound would you suggest?

### 2 'He goeth down' – stage direction line 43 (in pairs)

How does Romeo descend? As you go through the scene you'll see on page 129 that Juliet also 'goeth down' (stage direction, line 67). Work out how you would stage the scene to make these movements as convincing as possible. Prepare two suggestions, one for the Elizabethan stage (see page 214), and one for a staging of your own choice.

### 3 Juliet's vision (in groups of four)

The final words that the lovers speak together are filled with apprehension (lines 55–9). Prepare an enactment of these five lines, two of you as Romeo, two as Juliet. One pair delivers the lines the others present the vision each partner 'sees'.

Show your versions to the class. As you read to the end of the play, see how these dark forebodings work out.

---

**division** music (see how Juliet puns on 'divideth' in the next line. Notice too how Romeo puns on 'light' and 'dark' in line 36)
**affray** frighten (from each other's arms)

**hunt's-up** hunters' morning song
**ill-divining** evil-expecting
**dry sorrow** Elizabethans thought that each sigh cost a drop of blood

JULIET  It is, it is, hie hence, be gone, away!
It is the lark that sings so out of tune,
Straining harsh discords and unpleasing sharps.
Some say the lark makes sweet division:
This doth not so, for she divideth us.                           30
Some say the lark and loathèd toad changed eyes;
O now I would they had changed voices too,
Since arm from arm that voice doth us affray,
Hunting thee hence with hunt's-up to the day.
O now be gone, more light and light it grows.                    35
ROMEO  More light and light, more dark and dark our woes!

*Enter* NURSE [*hastily*].

NURSE  Madam!
JULIET  Nurse?
NURSE  Your lady mother is coming to your chamber.
The day is broke, be wary, look about.            [*Exit*]      40
JULIET  Then, window, let day in, and let life out.
ROMEO  Farewell, farewell! one kiss, and I'll descend.
                    [*He goeth down.*]
JULIET  Art thou gone so, love, lord, ay husband, friend?
I must hear from thee every day in the hour,
For in a minute there are many days.                             45
O, by this count I shall be much in years
Ere I again behold my Romeo!
ROMEO  [*From below*] Farewell!
I will omit no opportunity
That may convey my greetings, love, to thee.                     50
JULIET  O think'st thou we shall ever meet again?
ROMEO  I doubt it not, and all these woes shall serve
For sweet discourses in our times to come.
JULIET  O God, I have an ill-divining soul!
Methinks I see thee now, thou art so low,                        55
As one dead in the bottom of a tomb.
Either my eyesight fails, or thou look'st pale.
ROMEO  And trust me, love, in my eye so do you:
Dry sorrow drinks our blood. Adieu, adieu!        *Exit*

*Lady Capulet mistakes Juliet's tears for Romeo as grief for Tybalt's death. Juliet's replies strengthen her mother's mistaken belief, and she threatens vengeance, promising to have Romeo poisoned in Mantua.*

## 1 Fortune (individually or in pairs)

Juliet turns fortune into a person in lines 60–4. Imagine you are the designer for a production of the play. The director tells you that he wants an image or a statue of Fortune to be on stage throughout the play. Make drawings of your suggestions for that statue.

Talk together about whether you think the director's request for an always-present image is a good idea.

## 2 Double meanings (in groups of four)

Juliet's replies to her mother are filled with double meaning. Here's a way to bring this out: one person reads Lady Capulet, one reads Juliet (lines 68–102). The other two are Juliet's *alter ego*. They comment as many times as possible on what Juliet is really thinking as she speaks. Juliet reads slowly, a line or two at a time. For example:

Juliet: 'Madam, I am not well.'
*Alter ego*: 'Because I've just parted from my husband and my heart is full of sorrow' – and so on.

Try the exercise several times, changing roles. Discuss what these double meanings tell you about Juliet's character, and how they add to the dramatic impact of the play.

**asunder** apart
**runagate** runaway
**dram** poison

JULIET  O Fortune, Fortune, all men call thee fickle;                    60
      If thou art fickle, what dost thou with him
      That is renowned for faith? Be fickle, Fortune:
      For then I hope thou wilt not keep him long,
      But send him back.

              *Enter Mother* [LADY CAPULET *below*].

LADY CAPULET            Ho, daughter, are you up?
JULIET  Who is't that calls? It is my lady mother.                       65
      Is she not down so late, or up so early?
      What unaccustomed cause procures her hither?
      [*She goeth down from the window and enters below.*]
LADY CAPULET  Why how now, Juliet?
JULIET                 Madam, I am not well.
LADY CAPULET  Evermore weeping for your cousin's death?
      What, wilt thou wash him from his grave with tears?        70
      And if thou couldst, thou couldst not make him live;
      Therefore have done. Some grief shows much of love,
      But much of grief shows still some want of wit.
JULIET  Yet let me weep for such a feeling loss.
LADY CAPULET  So shall you feel the loss, but not the friend            75
      Which you weep for.
JULIET               Feeling so the loss,
      I cannot choose but ever weep the friend.
LADY CAPULET  Well, girl, thou weep'st not so much for his death
      As that the villain lives which slaughtered him.
JULIET  What villain, madam?
LADY CAPULET           That same villain Romeo.               80
JULIET  [*Aside*] Villain and he be many miles asunder. –
      God pardon him, I do with all my heart:
      And yet no man like he doth grieve my heart.
LADY CAPULET  That is because the traitor murderer lives.
JULIET  Ay, madam, from the reach of these my hands.                    85
      Would none but I might venge my cousin's death!
LADY CAPULET  We will have vengeance for it, fear thou not:
      Then weep no more. I'll send to one in Mantua,
      Where that same banished runagate doth live,
      Shall give him such an unaccustomed dram                   90
      That he shall soon keep Tybalt company;
      And then I hope thou wilt be satisfied.

*Lady Capulet tells Juliet that she must marry Paris on Thursday. Juliet, appalled, refuses to do so. Capulet comes in and mistakes Juliet's tears for sorrow for Tybalt.*

## 1 How to say the words? (in pairs)

Look at Juliet's 'in happy time' (line 111) and her mother's 'tell him so yourself' (line 124). How do you think those lines should be delivered?

To help you, read through lines 104–25, one person as Juliet, one as Lady Capulet. There are several things you could talk together about, but you might begin by asking: 'Is Juliet being sarcastic?' and 'Is her mother being callous and cruel?'

## 2 Fathers and daughters (in groups of four)

What does this arranged marriage suggest to you about male–female relationships in Verona?

If you are female, what would you do if you were suddenly told that your father had arranged a marriage for you to a man you barely know?

If you are male, do you think fathers should decide who their daughters should marry?

## 3 Capulet's language

As you read what Capulet says in this scene, notice how the tone and style of his language changes. He begins (lines 126–38) confidently offering fatherly comfort to Juliet. Trace how his language changes, and see how, in his second speech (lines 141–5), he talks of her in the third person ('she', 'her'). What do you think is the effect of this change?

---

**temper** mix (but Juliet also means weaken the poison to give Romeo peaceful sleep)
**wreak** avenge or bestow

**beseech** 'may I ask'
**ere** before
**conduit** water-pipe or fountain

JULIET  Indeed I never shall be satisfied
         With Romeo, till I behold him – dead –
         Is my poor heart, so for a kinsman vexed.                    95
         Madam, if you could find out but a man
         To bear a poison, I would temper it,
         That Romeo should upon receipt thereof
         Soon sleep in quiet. O how my heart abhors
         To hear him named and cannot come to him,                   100
         To wreak the love I bore my cousin
         Upon his body that hath slaughtered him!
LADY CAPULET  Find thou the means, and I'll find such a man.
         But now I'll tell thee joyful tidings, girl.
JULIET  And joy comes well in such a needy time.                      105
         What are they, beseech your ladyship?
LADY CAPULET  Well, well, thou hast a careful father, child,
         One who, to put thee from thy heaviness,
         Hath sorted out a sudden day of joy,
         That thou expects not, nor I looked not for.                110
JULIET  Madam, in happy time, what day is that?
LADY CAPULET  Marry, my child, early next Thursday morn,
         The gallant, young, and noble gentleman,
         The County Paris, at Saint Peter's Church,
         Shall happily make thee there a joyful bride.               115
JULIET  Now by Saint Peter's Church and Peter too,
         He shall not make me there a joyful bride.
         I wonder at this haste, that I must wed
         Ere he that should be husband comes to woo.
         I pray you tell my lord and father, madam,                  120
         I will not marry yet, and when I do, I swear
         It shall be Romeo, whom you know I hate,
         Rather than Paris. These are news indeed!
LADY CAPULET  Here comes your father, tell him so yourself;
         And see how he will take it at your hands.                  125

                    *Enter* CAPULET *and Nurse.*

CAPULET  When the sun sets, the earth doth drizzle dew,
         But for the sunset of my brother's son
         It rains downright.
         How now, a conduit, girl? What, still in tears?

*Capulet flies into a towering rage on hearing of Juliet's refusal to marry Paris. He threatens and insults her.*

## 1 Capulet's rage – how does Juliet feel?
(in groups of eight to twelve)

One person is Juliet, all the others are Capulet. Juliet sits still in the middle of a circle, the others all round her. Those reading Capulet will speak everything in lines 149–157, 160–8 and 176–95. The Capulets walk around Juliet and hurl their language at her. Each Capulet speaks just a phrase or a line or two before the next Capulet carries on. Juliet replies to every Capulet with her lines 158–9 ('Good father, I beseech you on my knees, Hear me with patience but to speak a word').

Work through the exercise several times, with a different Juliet each time. Remember that it's a difficult thing for Juliet to endure because she's on the receiving end of a terrifying tongue-lashing by her father. So don't force anyone into playing Juliet, only volunteers please!

When you've tried this activity a number of times, talk about the language. What's it like to undergo this verbal abuse? How does it feel to be delivering it?

This is an activity for the hall or drama studio, but it can also be adapted for the classroom.

## 2 Does Lady Capulet mean it?

'I would the fool were married to her grave' says Lady Capulet (line 140). Do you think she really means it? Is this another example of dramatic irony? (See page 122.)

---

**bark** ship
**chopt-logic** riddles
**minion** spoilt brat
**fettle your fine joints** get ready (the expression comes from grooming a horse)

**hurdle** frame on which prisoners were dragged to execution
**tallow** pale, waxy
**hilding** useless person

Evermore show'ring? In one little body                                    130
Thou counterfeits a bark, a sea, a wind:
For still thy eyes, which I may call the sea,
Do ebb and flow with tears; the bark thy body is,
Sailing in this salt flood; the winds, thy sighs,
Who, raging with thy tears and they with them,                            135
Without a sudden calm, will overset
Thy tempest-tossèd body. How now, wife,
Have you delivered to her our decree?

LADY CAPULET Ay, sir, but she will none, she gives you thanks.
I would the fool were married to her grave.                               140

CAPULET Soft, take me with you, take me with you, wife.
How, will she none? doth she not give us thanks?
Is she not proud? doth she not count her blest,
Unworthy as she is, that we have wrought
So worthy a gentleman to be her bride?                                    145

JULIET Not proud you have, but thankful that you have:
Proud can I never be of what I hate,
But thankful even for hate that is meant love.

CAPULET How how, how how, chopt-logic? What is this?
'Proud', and 'I thank you', and 'I thank you not',                        150
And yet 'not proud', mistress minion you?
Thank me no thankings, nor proud me no prouds,
But fettle your fine joints 'gainst Thursday next,
To go with Paris to Saint Peter's Church,
Or I will drag thee on a hurdle thither.                                  155
Out, you green-sickness carrion! out, you baggage!
You tallow-face!

LADY CAPULET             Fie, fie, what, are you mad?

JULIET Good father, I beseech you on my knees,
Hear me with patience but to speak a word.
[*She kneels down.*]

CAPULET Hang thee, young baggage, disobedient wretch!                     160
I tell thee what: get thee to church a'Thursday,
Or never after look me in the face.
Speak not, reply not, do not answer me!
My fingers itch. Wife, we scarce thought us blest
That God had lent us but this only child,                                 165
But now I see this one is one too much,
And that we have a curse in having her.
Out on her, hilding!

*Capulet, further enraged by the Nurse's defence of Juliet, continues to storm at Juliet, threatening to disown her if she will not obey him and marry Paris. Lady Capulet refuses to help her daughter.*

## 1 The power of fathers (in groups of five)

'And you be mine, I'll give you to my friend' (line 191).
'But and you will not wed, I'll pardon you' (line 187).
If you don't wed Paris, get out! says Capulet, using 'pardon' (forgive) ironically.

Talk together about what power fathers seemed to have over their daughters in Shakespeare's time, and what power they have now.

## 2 Juliet's appeal to her mother

'O sweet my mother, cast me not away' pleads Juliet (line 198).

Why do you think Lady Capulet replies as she does in lines 202–03?

## 3 What did the Capulets say to each other afterwards? (in pairs)

Imagine that Lady Capulet catches up with her husband shortly after leaving Juliet. What do they say to each other? Improvise their conversation.

## 4 An ominous image

Make a drawing to illustrate Juliet's prophecy in lines 200–01:

'. . . make the bridal bed
In that dim monument where Tybalt lies'.

---

**God-i-goden!** clear off! (mockingly: 'good-evening')
**gossip's bowl** drinks at a hen party
**God's bread** the sacred bread served at Mass (an oath)

**demesnes** lands
**puling** crying
**mammet** puppet
**be forsworn** be denied, break my oath

NURSE                    God in heaven bless her!
        You are to blame, my lord, to rate her so.
CAPULET  And why, my Lady Wisdom? Hold your tongue,          170
        Good Prudence, smatter with your gossips, go.
NURSE  I speak no treason.
CAPULET             O God-i-goden!
NURSE  May not one speak?
CAPULET             Peace, you mumbling fool!
        Utter your gravity o'er a gossip's bowl,
        For here we need it not.
LADY CAPULET             You are too hot.          175
CAPULET  God's bread, it makes me mad! Day, night, work, play,
        Alone, in company, still my care hath been
        To have her matched; and having now provided
        A gentleman of noble parentage,
        Of fair demesnes, youthful and nobly ligned,          180
        Stuffed, as they say, with honourable parts,
        Proportioned as one's thought would wish a man,
        And then to have a wretched puling fool,
        A whining mammet, in her fortune's tender,
        To answer 'I'll not wed, I cannot love;          185
        I am too young, I pray you pardon me.'
        But and you will not wed, I'll pardon you:
        Graze where you will, you shall not house with me.
        Look to't, think on't, I do not use to jest.
        Thursday is near, lay hand on heart, advise:          190
        And you be mine, I'll give you to my friend;
        And you be not, hang, beg, starve, die in the streets,
        For by my soul, I'll ne'er acknowledge thee,
        Nor what is mine shall never do thee good.
        Trust to't, bethink you, I'll not be forsworn.     *Exit*   195
JULIET  Is there no pity sitting in the clouds
        That sees into the bottom of my grief?
        O sweet my mother, cast me not away!
        Delay this marriage for a month, a week,
        Or if you do not, make the bridal bed          200
        In that dim monument where Tybalt lies.
LADY CAPULET  Talk not to me, for I'll not speak a word.
        Do as thou wilt, for I have done with thee.     *Exit*

*Juliet seeks comfort from the Nurse, who urges her to marry Paris. Feeling betrayed, Juliet sends the Nurse away, vowing never to trust her again. Juliet resolves to seek Friar Lawrence's aid.*

## 1 Juliet and the Nurse (in pairs)

Read or act out lines 204–42, one person as Juliet, one as the Nurse. Afterwards, talk together about:

- what you think of the Nurse's advice
- whether you think the Nurse recognises Juliet's irony or sarcasm when she says 'Amen' and 'Well, thou hast comforted me marvellous much'
- what the Nurse's advice adds to your knowledge of her character
- how your understanding of Juliet has grown in this scene
- what you think would be the most dramatically effective way of staging these lines.

## 2 What was the Nurse's news? (in groups of four)

Imagine the Nurse meets three of her friends. They are eager to know what happened in the Capulet household that day. How does their conversation go? Remember that this group is probably what Capulet had in mind when he spoke dismissively of 'a gossip's bowl' (line 174).

## 3 The noose tightens on Juliet

Notice how Juliet increasingly feels trapped. Not only are her parents threatening her, but her religion adds to her dilemma. In lines 205–8 she recognises that only by Romeo's death can she sincerely take a faithful (religious) vow to marry Paris.

---

**stratagems** tricks
**green** green eyes were thought to be especially admirable
**beshrew** curse

**absolved** forgiven
**bosom** secret thoughts
**twain** two (separated)

JULIET  O God! – O Nurse, how shall this be prevented?
My husband is on earth, my faith in heaven;               205
How shall that faith return again to earth,
Unless that husband send it me from heaven
By leaving earth? Comfort me, counsel me.
Alack, alack, that heaven should practise stratagems
Upon so soft a subject as myself!                         210
What say'st thou? hast thou not a word of joy?
Some comfort, Nurse.
NURSE                      Faith, here it is:
Romeo is banished, and all the world to nothing
That he dares ne'er come back to challenge you;
Or if he do, it needs must be by stealth.                 215
Then since the case so stands as now it doth,
I think it best you married with the County.
O, he's a lovely gentleman!
Romeo's a dishclout to him. An eagle, madam,
Hath not so green, so quick, so fair an eye               220
As Paris hath. Beshrew my very heart,
I think you are happy in this second match,
For it excels your first, or if it did not,
Your first is dead, or 'twere as good he were
As living here and you no use of him.                     225
JULIET  Speak'st thou from thy heart?
NURSE  And from my soul too, else beshrew them both.
JULIET  Amen.
NURSE  What?
JULIET  Well, thou hast comforted me marvellous much.     230
Go in, and tell my lady I am gone,
Having displeased my father, to Lawrence' cell,
To make confession and to be absolved.
NURSE  Marry, I will, and this is wisely done.   [Exit]
JULIET  [She looks after Nurse.]
Ancient damnation! O most wicked fiend!                   235
Is it more sin to wish me thus forsworn,
Or to dispraise my lord with that same tongue
Which she hath praised him with above compare
So many thousand times? Go, counsellor,
Thou and my bosom henceforth shall be twain.              240
I'll to the Friar to know his remedy;
If all else fail, myself have power to die.    Exit

# Looking back at Act 3
*Activities for groups or individuals*

## 1 Set the Act in your school

Choose five sites, somewhere in or around the school, where the five scenes of Act 3 could most suitably be staged. Present your suggestions to the class, together with your reasons for the appropriateness of each site for each scene.

## 2 Newspaper billboards or soundbites

Newspaper billboards give very brief summaries of the news. Write five of them, one for each scene. Each billboard should catch the heart of the action of each scene.

Or try soundbites: very short clips, used on television or radio, of what someone has said. Make up soundbites for each scene, partly in Shakespeare's language, partly in your own. Each soundbite is ten seconds or shorter.

## 3 Your own soap? ... an improvisation

Update one scene on this act. Choose a modern 'soap opera' (a familiar series on television). Write and act out your own episode, based on Shakespeare's scene, in the style of that 'soap'.

## 4 Design a 'wanted' poster

Romeo is banished on pain of death. Design the poster that is pasted up on the walls of Verona to announce his sentence.

## 5 Characters' motives?

List each character who appears in this act. Write a single sentence for each which begins 'What I want most is ...'. How much agreement is there in the class on each character's major motive?

## 6 Banishment – three questions

- Is there a modern equivalent of the punishment of banishment?
- Is banishment really worse than death as Romeo imagines?
- Why doesn't Juliet simply decide to join Romeo in Mantua?

## 7 Do you identify with a character?

You've now met all the major characters in the play. With which of the characters do you most identify? Write down some of the reasons why you feel in tune with that character.

With which character do you least identify – and why?

## 8 Guess the incident – or the line

Select an incident or line from the act and prepare a short mime or a tableau. Tell the class from which scene you have chosen the event or line. Then show your mime or tableau. If the other groups can guess the incident or line correctly, that's a compliment to their perception and to your ability in performance!

## 9 First words . . .

Read aloud the first four lines only of each scene. Do this several times, then talk together about the differences between the language of each. How far do you think these 'openings' set the mood of each scene?

## 10 . . . and last words

Say aloud the final word in each scene. Do this several times, then make up your own short play, in five scenes that ends with those same words.

## 11 'A plague a' both your houses!'

Mercutio, at the point of death, curses the Capulets and Montagues alike. As you read through the play keep his dying words in mind to see how his curse comes true.

## 12 Caption the Act – for a children's comic

Make a cartoon drawing (use 'stick men and women' if you can't draw well) for each of the five scenes. Underneath each write a caption in language that you think is suitable for six- or seven-year-olds. Each caption should describe the central action of each scene.

*Paris tells Friar Lawrence that Capulet, believing Juliet is grieving for Tybalt, wishes to have her married soon. Capulet thinks an early marriage will ease her sorrow.*

Royal Shakespeare Theatre, 1961. This is the only time Paris and Juliet meet in the play. Do you think they have met earlier?

## 1 'What must be shall be'

What do you think Juliet means by her remark in line 21? It echoes one of the major themes running through the play (see page 204).

**my father Capulet** Paris already thinks of Capulet as his father-in-law to be

**Venus** Goddess of love
**society** company, companionship

# ACT 4 SCENE 1
## Friar Lawrence's cell

*Enter* FRIAR LAWRENCE *and* COUNTY PARIS.

FRIAR LAWRENCE On Thursday, sir? the time is very short.
PARIS My father Capulet will have it so,
    And I am nothing slow to slack his haste.
FRIAR LAWRENCE You say you do not know the lady's mind?
    Uneven is the course, I like it not.          5
PARIS Immoderately she weeps for Tybalt's death,
    And therefore have I little talked of love,
    For Venus smiles not in a house of tears.
    Now, sir, her father counts it dangerous
    That she do give her sorrow so much sway;     10
    And in his wisdom hastes our marriage
    To stop the inundation of her tears,
    Which too much minded by herself alone
    May be put from her by society.
    Now do you know the reason of this haste.     15
FRIAR LAWRENCE [*Aside*]
    I would I knew not why it should be slowed. –
    Look, sir, here comes the lady toward my cell.

*Enter* JULIET.

PARIS Happily met, my lady and my wife!
JULIET That may be, sir, when I may be a wife.
PARIS That 'may be' must be, love, on Thursday next.     20
JULIET What must be shall be.
FRIAR LAWRENCE               That's a certain text.

*Juliet's replies to Paris are filled with double meaning. After Paris leaves, Juliet asks Friar Lawrence for help, threatening to kill herself is she is forced to marry Paris.*

### 1 How do Paris and Juliet talk together? (in pairs)

Read aloud lines 18–43, one person as Paris, the other as Juliet (leave out Friar Lawrence's lines). Experiment with different ways of speaking your character. For example, first read Paris' lines tenderly and courteously. Then speak his lines as if he were officious, having no regard for Juliet's feelings, but treating her as a mere possession. Also explore about different ways of how Juliet might speak.

Talk together about your different styles of speaking. Can you agree which tones and attitudes are most appropriate for each character?

### 2 'Come weep with me, past hope, past cure, past help!'

Write your own poem. Take line 45 as the opening line. You may wish to make your poem express Juliet's plight – or to use the line as the beginning of a free-ranging poem. If you wish to write your poem as a sonnet see page 211.

### 3 Actions and words

What does Juliet *do* with the knife as she speaks lines 50–9?

**pensive** sad (but would Paris' view of Juliet's sadness be different from the Friar's?)
**the compass of my wits** the range of my understanding

**prorogue** delay
**label** seal (on a legal document)

PARIS  Come you to make confession to this father?
JULIET  To answer that, I should confess to you.
PARIS  Do not deny to him that you love me.
JULIET  I will confess to you that I love him.                    25
PARIS  So will ye, I am sure, that you love me.
JULIET  If I do so, it will be of more price,
        Being spoke behind your back, than to your face.
PARIS  Poor soul, thy face is much abused with tears.
JULIET  The tears have got small victory by that,              30
        For it was bad enough before their spite.
PARIS  Thou wrong'st it more than tears with that report.
JULIET  That is no slander, sir, which is a truth,
        And what I spake, I spake it to my face.
PARIS  Thy face is mine, and thou hast slandered it.            35
JULIET  It may be so, for it is not mine own.
        Are you at leisure, holy father, now,
        Or shall I come to you at evening mass?
FRIAR LAWRENCE  My leisure serves me, pensive daughter, now.
        My lord, we must entreat the time alone.                 40
PARIS  God shield I should disturb devotion!
        Juliet, on Thursday early will I rouse ye;
        Till then adieu, and keep this holy kiss.      *Exit*
JULIET  O shut the door, and when thou hast done so,
        Come weep with me, past hope, past cure, past help!    45
FRIAR LAWRENCE  O Juliet, I already know thy grief,
        It strains me past the compass of my wits.
        I hear thou must, and nothing may prorogue it,
        On Thursday next be married to this County.
JULIET  Tell me not, Friar, that thou hearest of this,         50
        Unless thou tell me how I may prevent it.
        If in thy wisdom thou canst give no help,
        Do thou but call my resolution wise,
        And with this knife I'll help it presently.
        God joined my heart and Romeo's, thou our hands,       55
        And ere this hand, by thee to Romeo's sealed,
        Shall be the label to another deed,
        Or my true heart with treacherous revolt
        Turn to another, this shall slay them both:

*Friar Lawrence begins to devise a plan to prevent Juliet's marriage to Paris. Juliet declares that she will do anything to escape the wedding.*

---

## 1 'Rather than marry Paris' (in groups of three to five)

Lines 77–86 list at least six things Juliet says she is prepared to do rather than marry Paris. Work out a mime to show six or more of the actions she describes.

Talk together about some of the things you would rather do than marry someone not of your own choice. Write your own list, matching it as closely to Juliet's as possible. Present a mime of your preferred actions to the rest of the class, to see if they can guess what you would rather do!

## 2 The charnel-house

Most Elizabethan graveyards had a charnel-house. It was a building where bones and skulls were stacked after they were dug up when fresh graves were being prepared for new burials. In Shakespeare's time, Stratford-upon-Avon churchyard possessed a large charnel-house. Write a poem or a short story with the title 'The charnel-house'. You may wish to use some of Juliet's language.

---

commission authority
issue outcome
cop'st with meet and struggle with

reeky shanks stinking legbones
chapless without a jawbone

Therefore, out of thy long-experienced time,                     60
Give me some present counsel, or, behold,
'Twixt my extremes and me this bloody knife
Shall play the umpire, arbitrating that
Which the commission of thy years and art
Could to no issue of true honour bring.                          65
Be not so long to speak, I long to die,
If what thou speak'st speak not of remedy.
FRIAR LAWRENCE Hold, daughter, I do spy a kind of hope,
Which craves as desperate an execution
As that is desperate which we would prevent.                     70
If, rather than to marry County Paris,
Thou hast the strength of will to slay thyself,
Then is it likely thou wilt undertake
A thing like death to chide away this shame,
That cop'st with Death himself to scape from it;                 75
And if thou dar'st, I'll give thee remedy.
JULIET O bid me leap, rather than marry Paris,
From off the battlements of any tower,
Or walk in thievish ways, or bid me lurk
Where serpents are; chain me with roaring bears,                 80
Or hide me nightly in a charnel-house,
O'ercovered quite with dead men's rattling bones,
With reeky shanks and yellow chapless skulls;
Or bid me go into a new-made grave,
And hide me with a dead man in his shroud –                      85
Things that to hear them told have made me tremble –
And I will do it without fear or doubt,
To live an unstained wife to my sweet love.
FRIAR LAWRENCE Hold then, go home, be merry, give consent
To marry Paris. Wednesday is tomorrow;                           90
Tomorrow night look that thou lie alone,
Let not the Nurse lie with thee in thy chamber.

*Friar Lawrence explains his plan. He will give Juliet a potion to make her seem dead. She will be placed in the Capulet vault, Romeo will be with her when she awakens to take her to Mantua.*

## 1 What do you think of the Friar's plan? (in pairs)

Read the Friar's plan to each other (lines 89–117) in sections, one small part at a time, like this: 'Hold then', 'go home', 'give consent to marry Paris', . . . 'Take thou this vial', 'being then in bed', 'And this distilling liquor drink thou off' . . ., etc.

As one person reads each small section, the other mimes the actions. Do this twice. When you understand what the Friar is proposing, talk together about what you think of his scheme.

## 2 Make up your own plan to help Juliet!

Work out a plan of your own to help Juliet resolve her troubles. Make it as improbable as you like, but (like the Friar's) with some chance of succeeding – if everything goes right. Share your plan with the class.

## 3 What are the Friar's motives? (in groups of four)

From all your knowledge of him so far, talk together about what you think of the Friar. Explore why he works out such a complicated and dangerous plan. What are his motives? Juliet trusts him – do you think she is wise to take the risk?

## 4 Juliet's character in this scene (in groups of four)

Look back through all that Juliet has said in this scene. What more does her language add to your knowledge of her character?

---

**vial** small bottle
**humour** fluid
**no pulse . . . surcease** your pulse will stop beating
**wanny** pale

**supple government** easy movement
**against** before
**drift** purpose or plan
**toy** whim, trifle

Take thou this vial, being then in bed,
And this distilling liquor drink thou off,
When presently through all thy veins shall run                     95
A cold and drowsy humour; for no pulse
Shall keep his native progress, but surcease;
No warmth, no breath shall testify thou livest;
The roses in thy lips and cheeks shall fade
To wanny ashes, thy eyes' windows fall,                            100
Like Death when he shuts up the day of life;
Each part, deprived of supple government,
Shall stiff and stark and cold appear like death,
And in this borrowed likeness of shrunk death
Thou shalt continue two and forty hours,                           105
And then awake as from a pleasant sleep.
Now when the bridegroom in the morning comes
To rouse thee from thy bed, there art thou dead.
Then as the manner of our country is,
In thy best robes, uncovered on the bier,                          110
Thou shall be borne to that same ancient vault
Where all the kindred of the Capulets lie.
In the mean time, against thou shalt awake,
Shall Romeo by my letters know our drift,
And hither shall he come, and he and I                             115
Will watch thy waking, and that very night
Shall Romeo bear thee hence to Mantua.
And this shall free thee from this present shame,
If no inconstant toy, nor womanish fear,
Abate thy valour in the acting it.                                 120
JULIET  Give me, give me! O tell not me of fear.
FRIAR LAWRENCE  Hold, get you gone, be strong and prosperous
          In this resolve; I'll send a friar with speed
          To Mantua, with my letters to thy lord.
JULIET  Love give me strength, and strength shall help afford.     125
          Farewell, dear father.
                                                    *Exeunt*

*Capulet is busy with the wedding preparations. Juliet enters and begs forgiveness. She promises to obey him in future.*

---

## 1 Preparations for the wedding (in groups of four)

Talk together about the opening nine lines. Why do you think Shakespeare included this little scene of life in the Capulet household?

## 2 'How now, my headstrong' (in groups of three)

Try saying this line aloud in as many ways as you can. Can you agree about how you think it should be said? What more does it tell you about Capulet's character?

Capulet in the Royal Shakespeare Company's 1973 production.

---

servingmen  in modern productions, usually played by Peter, Sampson and Gregory
unfurnished  unprepared

harlotry  hussy, good-for-nothing
shrift  confession
behests  commands

# ACT 4    SCENE 2
## Capulet's mansion

*Enter Father* CAPULET, *Mother* [LADY CAPULET], NURSE, *and*
SERVINGMEN, *two or three.*

CAPULET  So many guests invite as here are writ.
                                      *[Exit Servingman]*
    Sirrah, go hire me twenty cunning cooks.

SERVINGMAN  You shall have none ill, sir, for I'll try if they can lick
    their fingers.

CAPULET  How canst thou try them so?                  5

SERVINGMAN  Marry, sir, 'tis an ill cook that cannot lick his own
    fingers; therefore he that cannot lick his fingers goes not with me.

CAPULET  Go, be gone.
                                      *[Exit Servingman]*
    We shall be much unfurnished for this time.
    What, is my daughter gone to Friar Lawrence?    10

NURSE  Ay forsooth.

CAPULET  Well, he may chance to do some good on her.
    A peevish self-willed harlotry it is.

*Enter* JULIET.

NURSE  See where she comes from shrift with merry look.

CAPULET  How now, my headstrong, where have you been gadding?    15

JULIET  Where I have learnt me to repent the sin
    Of disobedient opposition
    To you and your behests, and am enjoined
    By holy Lawrence to fall prostrate here
    To beg your pardon.
                                      *[She kneels down.]*
                Pardon, I beseech you!    20
    Henceforward I am ever ruled by you.

*Capulet is delighted by Juliet's submission. He decides she shall be married tomorrow, and will manage all the wedding arrangements himself.*

## 1 Juliet's lies (in groups of four)

Look closely at everything Juliet says in this short scene. Judge each part as to whether you think it 'true' or 'false'.

One person reads Juliet's words aloud whilst the others say 'true' or 'false' for each small section of what she says.

Talk together about what you think of Juliet's behaviour here. Does it alter your feelings about her in any way?

## 2 Dramatic irony (in pairs)

'Dramatic irony' is when the audience knows something that at least one of the characters on stage does not know.

Go through the lines opposite, picking out as many examples of dramatic irony as you can.

From your list, choose two that you think are the most powerful examples of dramatic irony. Can you make up a short dramatic presentation of what you've found to show to the class?

## 3 Capulet's haste (something to think about)

Notice how Capulet brings forward the wedding day from Thursday to Wednesday ('tomorrow morning'). How important is this in accelerating the tragedy? (see page 206)

**becomèd**  proper or appropriate
**bound**  indebted
**deck up**  dress

CAPULET  Send for the County, go tell him of this.
　　　　　I'll have this knot knit up tomorrow morning.
JULIET  I met the youthful lord at Lawrence' cell,
　　　　　And gave him what becomèd love I might,　　　　　　　25
　　　　　Not stepping o'er the bounds of modesty.
CAPULET  Why, I am glad on't, this is well, stand up.
　　　　　This is as't should be. Let me see the County;
　　　　　Ay, marry, go, I say, and fetch him hither.
　　　　　Now afore God, this reverend holy Friar,　　　　　　　30
　　　　　All our whole city is much bound to him.
JULIET  Nurse, will you go with me into my closet,
　　　　　To help me sort such needful ornaments
　　　　　As you think fit to furnish me tomorrow?
LADY CAPULET  No, not till Thursday, there is time enough.　　35
CAPULET  Go, Nurse, go with her, we'll to church tomorrow.
　　　　　　　　　　　　　　　　*Exeunt* [*Juliet and Nurse*]
LADY CAPULET  We shall be short in our provision,
　　　　　'Tis now near night.
CAPULET　　　　　　　　　　Tush, I will stir about,
　　　　　And all things shall be well, I warrant thee, wife:
　　　　　Go thou to Juliet, help to deck up her;　　　　　　　40
　　　　　I'll not to bed tonight; let me alone,
　　　　　I'll play the huswife for this once. What ho!
　　　　　They are all forth. Well, I will walk myself
　　　　　To County Paris, to prepare up him
　　　　　Against tomorrow. My heart is wondrous light,　　　　45
　　　　　Since this same wayward girl is so reclaimed.
　　　　　　　　　　　　　　　　　　　　　　*Exeunt*

*Juliet sends her Nurse and mother away. Alone, she fights her fears, plucking up courage to drink the 'poison'. If it does not work she will kill herself with a dagger rather than be married.*

## 1 Juliet's thoughts (in pairs)

Juliet deliberately deceives her mother and the Nurse. In lines 1–12, she once again uses language rich in double meanings and dramatic irony. This short exercise explores what may be in her mind. One person reads aloud everything Juliet says up to line 12. Read only a short section at a time, then pause. In each pause, your partner says aloud what Juliet is really thinking. Read again, changing roles.

Talk together about how this adds to your understanding of Juliet's character, and of her feelings about her mother and the Nurse.

## 2 Shakespeare's imagination at work

Lines 1–12 opposite are Shakespeare's re-writing of a section of a long poem by Arthur Brooke, *The Tragical History of Romeus and Juliet* (1562). What differences can you find between Shakespeare's version and the original below?

'Unto her chamber doth the pensive wight repair
And in her hand a percher light the Nurse bears up the stair.
In Juliet's chamber was her wonted use to lie,
Wherefore her mistress dreading that she should her work descry
As soon as she began her pallet to unfold
Thinking to lie that night, where she was wont to lie of old,
Doth gently pray her seek her lodging somewhere else.'

Find a copy of Brooke's poem (e.g. in the *New Cambridge Shakespeare* edition of the play). Compare it with *Romeo and Juliet*. You'll be surprised at how closely Shakespeare follows many passages. But see how his language and imagination transform them! (There's more about this on page 213.)

---

**attires** clothes
**orisons** prayers

**culled** picked out
**behoveful** appropriate

# ACT 4   SCENE 3
## Juliet's bedroom

*Enter* JULIET *and* NURSE.

JULIET  Ay, those attires are best, but, gentle Nurse,
I pray thee leave me to myself tonight:
For I have need of many orisons
To move the heavens to smile upon my state,
Which, well thou knowest, is cross and full of sin.                    5

*Enter Mother* [LADY CAPULET].

LADY CAPULET  What, are you busy, ho? need you my help?
JULIET  No, madam, we have culled such necessaries
As are behoveful for our state tomorrow.
So please you, let me now be left alone,
And let the Nurse this night sit up with you,                          10
For I am sure you have your hands full all,
In this so sudden business.
LADY CAPULET                                       Good night.
Get thee to bed and rest, for thou hast need.
*Exeunt* [*Lady Capulet and Nurse*]
JULIET  Farewell! God knows when we shall meet again.
I have a faint cold fear thrills through my veins                      15
That almost freezes up the heat of life:
I'll call them back again to comfort me.
Nurse! – What should she do here?
My dismal scene I needs must act alone.
Come, vial.                                                            20
What if this mixture do not work at all?
Shall I be married then tomorrow morning?
No, no, this shall forbid it; lie thou there.
[*Laying down her dagger.*]

*Juliet is filled with fearful thoughts. Is the Friar honest? Will she awake in the tomb before Romeo comes? Will she go mad with dread? She drinks the potion.*

## 1 Juliet's fears (lines 15–58)

Try one or more of the following:

a **Radio play** (in groups of four to five)
Treat the lines as a radio play for voices. Add sound effects, record your final version.

b **Atmosphere** (whole class)
Share out the lines. Everyone takes at least one line and learns it by heart. Then, kneeling in a circle, the class speaks the whole speech, building up as tense and dramatic an atmosphere as possible.

c **Sequence** (in small groups)
Break the speech into sections, e.g. lines 15–19; lines 20–3; lines 24–9; lines 30–5; lines 36–54; lines 55–7; line 58. Work out some way of presenting each section to show the progression of Juliet's fears.

Don't be afraid to give your imagination full rein as you try to catch Juliet's thoughts and feelings. Make up your own way of expressing these final words before she drinks the 'poison'.

d **Echoes** (in pairs)
Take lines 30–57. One person reads the lines. The other echoes every word to do with fear or death. What does this exercise tell you about Juliet's feelings?

e **Staging** (in groups of three)
Direct the scene for the Elizabethan stage pictured on page 214.

Work out the suggestions you would give to Juliet to help her deliver lines 15–58 on that stage. Also, work out how to stage the scene on a modern stage. What differences emerge?

---

**ministered** administered, given
**tried** proved
**conceit** thought

**mandrakes** plants that were believed to grow beneath gallows and to shriek as they were pulled up
**Environèd** surrounded
**spit** pierce

What if it be a poison which the Friar
Subtly hath ministered to have me dead,                    25
Lest in this marriage he should be dishonoured,
Because he married me before to Romeo?
I fear it is, and yet methinks it should not,
For he hath still been tried a holy man.
How if, when I am laid into the tomb,                      30
I wake before the time that Romeo
Come to redeem me? There's a fearful point!
Shall I not then be stifled in the vault,
To whose foul mouth no healthsome air breathes in,
And there die strangled ere my Romeo comes?               35
Or if I live, is it not very like
The horrible conceit of death and night,
Together with the terror of the place –
As in a vault, an ancient receptacle,
Where for this many hundred years the bones                40
Of all my buried ancestors are packed,
Where bloody Tybalt, yet but green in earth,
Lies fest'ring in his shroud, where, as they say,
At some hours in the night spirits resort –
Alack, alack, is it not like that I,                       45
So early waking – what with loathsome smells,
And shrieks like mandrakes' torn out of the earth,
That living mortals hearing them run mad –
O, if I wake, shall I not be distraught,
Environèd with all these hideous fears,                    50
And madly play with my forefathers' joints,
And pluck the mangled Tybalt from his shroud,
And in this rage, with some great kinsman's bone,
As with a club, dash out my desp'rate brains?
O look! methinks I see my cousin's ghost                   55
Seeking out Romeo that did spit his body
Upon a rapier's point. Stay, Tybalt, stay!
Romeo, Romeo, Romeo! Here's drink – I drink to thee.
    [*She falls upon her bed, within the curtains.*]

*The wedding preparations are well under way.*

---

### 1 Angelica – What's the Nurse's name? (in pairs)

No one is quite sure whether Angelica is the Nurse's name or Lady Capulet's. In the 1992 production by the Royal Shakespeare Company, Angelica was a young serving-woman with whom Capulet was obviously having an affair. Talk together about who you think Capulet is calling Angelica. It may be helpful to know that for Shakespeare, Angelica probably meant 'beautiful princess'.

No one's quite sure either about whether the Nurse or Lady Capulet speaks lines 6–8. Who do you think is most likely to speak them?

### 2 Husband and wife (in groups of four)

Talk together about why you think Lady Capulet says lines 11–12 to her husband. What is her tone of voice? Improvise a conversation between two servants in which they talk about the past and present relationship of Capulet and his wife.

### 3 Watching

Notice how all three characters play on the word 'watch' (lines 7–12). Can you work out the various meanings in their punning?

---

**pastry** part of the kitchen where pastry was made
**curfew bell** bell announcing daylight

**cot-quean** man who does woman's work
**mouse-hunt** woman-chaser
**hood** woman

# ACT 4   SCENE 4
## A room in Capulet's mansion

*Enter lady of the house* LADY CAPULET *and* NURSE *with herbs.*

LADY CAPULET  Hold, take these keys and fetch more spices, Nurse.
NURSE  They call for dates and quinces in the pastry.

*Enter old* CAPULET.

CAPULET  Come, stir, stir, stir! the second cock hath crowed,
    The curfew bell hath rung, 'tis three a'clock.
    Look to the baked meats, good Angelica,         5
    Spare not for cost.
NURSE                Go, you cot-quean, go,
    Get you to bed. Faith, you'll be sick tomorrow
    For this night's watching.
CAPULET  No, not a whit. What, I have watched ere now
    All night for lesser cause, and ne'er been sick.       10
LADY CAPULET  Ay, you have been a mouse-hunt in your time,
    But I will watch you from such watching now.
                 *Exeunt Lady [Capulet] and Nurse*
CAPULET  A jealous hood, a jealous hood!

*Enter three or four [*SERVINGMEN*] with spits and logs and
baskets.*
                      Now, fellow,
    What is there?
FIRST SERVINGMAN  Things for the cook, sir, but I know not what.   15

Romeo and Juliet

*Capulet fusses busily with the wedding arrangements. He tells the Nurse to wake Juliet. The next scene opens with the Nurse attempting to rouse Juliet.*

---

## 1 Master and servants

- What action do you think the servant makes when he says 'I have a head, sir, that will find out logs'?
- What does this scene show about master and servant relationships in Capulet's household?
- Why do you think Shakespeare places this scene between the serious ones that precede and follow it?

## 2 Make the scene flow (in pairs)

Scenes 3, 4 and 5 are set in Capulet's mansion (in Juliet's bedroom and another room). How could you ensure that the stage action flows smoothly throughout these scenes?

Work out how that 'flow' can be achieved in these three scenes – on both the Elizabethan stage (see page 214) and on a modern one. The stage directions will help you (e.g. for Juliet at the end of Scene 3: 'She falls upon her bed, within the curtains').

---

**whoreson** bastard (Do you think Capulet says this seriously or jokingly?)

**loggerhead** blockhead (but 'loggerheads' also means 'quarrel' or 'dispute', one of the themes of the play. See pages 204 and 206.)

CAPULET Make haste, make haste.

> *[Exit First Servingman]*

    Sirrah, fetch drier logs.

Call Peter, he will show thee where they are.

SECOND SERVINGMAN I have a head, sir, that will find out logs,

    And never trouble Peter for the matter.

CAPULET Mass, and well said, a merry whoreson, ha!      20

    Thou shalt be loggerhead.

> *[Exeunt Second Servingman and any others]*

    Good faith, 'tis day.

The County will be here with music straight,

For so he said he would.

> *(Play music [within].)*

    I hear him near.

Nurse! Wife! What ho! What, Nurse, I say!

> *Enter Nurse.*

Go waken Juliet, go and trim her up,      25

I'll go and chat with Paris. Hie, make haste,

Make haste, the bridegroom he is come already,

Make haste, I say.     *[Exit]*


# ACT 4   SCENE 5
## Juliet's bedroom

NURSE Mistress, what mistress! Juliet! Fast, I warrant her, she.

    Why, lamb! why, lady! fie, you slug-a-bed!

    Why, love, I say! madam! sweet heart! why, bride!

    What, not a word? You take your pennyworths now;

    Sleep for a week, for the next night I warrant      5

    The County Paris hath set up his rest

    That you shall rest but little. God forgive me!

Romeo and Juliet

*The Nurse, thinking Juliet to be dead, raises the house with her cries. Lady Capulet and her husband express their grief. Paris, unaware, enters to take Juliet to church.*

## 1 The Nurse's changing moods (in pairs)

Read lines 1–16 to each other, trying out different ways of saying each line. Can you agree on a version you prefer? Work out the actions and movements you would use to accompany the Nurse's words. Decide whether your version includes a 'sudden' or 'gradual' realisation by the Nurse of Juliet's death.

## 2 Friar Lawrence's entrance – something to think about

Friar Lawrence enters with Paris and the musicians. He alone knows Juliet is not dead. How would he say line 33 – and what's he really thinking at that moment?

## 3 'Death lies on her like an untimely frost Upon the sweetest flower of all the field'

Make a drawing or write a poem or story to show what the lines mean to you.

aqua-vitae brandy

Marry and amen! How sound is she asleep!
I needs must wake her. Madam, madam, madam!
Ay, let the County take you in your bed,                    10
He'll fright you up, i'faith. Will it not be?
           [*Draws back the curtains.*]
What, dressed, and in your clothes, and down again?
I must needs wake you. Lady, lady, lady!
Alas, alas! Help, help! my lady's dead!
O weraday that ever I was born!                            15
Some aqua-vitae, ho! My lord! My lady!

           [*Enter Mother,* LADY CAPULET.]

LADY CAPULET  What noise is here?
NURSE                              O lamentable day!
LADY CAPULET  What is the matter?
NURSE                              Look, look! O heavy day!
LADY CAPULET  O me, O me, my child, my only life!
           Revive, look up, or I will die with thee.        20
           Help, help! Call help.

           *Enter Father* [CAPULET].

CAPULET  For shame, bring Juliet forth, her lord is come.
NURSE  She's dead, deceased, she's dead, alack the day!
LADY CAPULET  Alack the day, she's dead, she's dead, she's dead!
CAPULET  Hah, let me see her. Out alas, she's cold,         25
           Her blood is settled, and her joints are stiff:
           Life and these lips have long been separated;
           Death lies on her like an untimely frost
           Upon the sweetest flower of all the field.
NURSE  O lamentable day!
LADY CAPULET           O woeful time!                        30
CAPULET  Death that hath tane her hence to make me wail
           Ties up my tongue and will not let me speak.

           *Enter* FRIAR [LAWRENCE] *and the* COUNTY [PARIS *with the*
                      MUSICIANS].

FRIAR LAWRENCE  Come, is the bride ready to go to church?

*The Capulets, the Nurse, and Paris mourn for Juliet. The Friar attempts to offer consolation.*

---

## 1 Mourning for Juliet (in groups of four)

Each person takes a part: Capulet, Paris, Lady Capulet, the Nurse. Read aloud lines 35–64. Change parts and read again. Change again until everyone has read all four parts.

Talk together about the different ways in which the four characters express their grief over the 'dead' Juliet.

Critics of the play have said that some of the mourning is selfish, artificial and self-indulgent. Do you agree with that view? Work out a statement about each character to show how the way in which they mourn matches their personality.

## 2 What does the audience feel?

What is the effect on an audience of this scene of mourning? After all, the audience knows that Juliet is alive, not dead.

## 3 'In lasting labour of his pilgrimage' (in pairs)

In lines 44–5 Lady Capulet personifies time. She turns 'time' into a pilgrim toiling unceasingly through each day. But what is the purpose of time's journeying here? Prepare a short mime to show time as a person and talk together about his possible destinations. (See also page 206.)

CAPULET Ready to go, but never to return. –
　　　　O son, the night before thy wedding day　　　　35
　　　　Hath Death lain with thy wife. There she lies,
　　　　Flower as she was, deflowerèd by him.
　　　　Death is my son-in-law, Death is my heir,
　　　　My daughter he hath wedded. I will die,
　　　　And leave him all; life, living, all is Death's.　　40
PARIS Have I thought long to see this morning's face,
　　　　And doth it give me such a sight as this?
LADY CAPULET Accursed, unhappy, wretched, hateful day!
　　　　Most miserable hour that e'er time saw
　　　　In lasting labour of his pilgrimage!　　　　45
　　　　But one, poor one, one poor and loving child,
　　　　But one thing to rejoice and solace in,
　　　　And cruel Death hath catched it from my sight!
NURSE O woe! O woeful, woeful, woeful day!
　　　　Most lamentable day, most woeful day　　　　50
　　　　That ever, ever, I did yet behold!
　　　　O day, O day, O day, O hateful day!
　　　　Never was seen so black a day as this.
　　　　O woeful day, O woeful day!
PARIS Beguiled, divorcèd, wrongèd, spited, slain!　　55
　　　　Most detestable Death, by thee beguiled,
　　　　By cruel, cruel thee quite overthrown!
　　　　O love! O life! not life, but love in death!
CAPULET Despised, distressèd, hated, martyred, killed!
　　　　Uncomfortable time, why cam'st thou now　　60
　　　　To murder, murder our solemnity?
　　　　O child, O child! my soul, and not my child!
　　　　Dead art thou. Alack, my child is dead,
　　　　And with my child my joys are burièd.
FRIAR LAWRENCE Peace ho, for shame! Confusion's cure lives not　65
　　　　In these confusions. Heaven and yourself
　　　　Had part in this fair maid, now heaven hath all,
　　　　And all the better is it for the maid:
　　　　Your part in her you could not keep from death,
　　　　But heaven keeps his part in eternal life.　　70

163

*Friar Lawrence rebukes the family for their grief. They should stop crying because Juliet is now in heaven. He tells them to prepare her funeral. Everyone leaves except Peter and the musicians.*

## 1 The Friar's secret thoughts (in pairs)

The Friar knows Juliet is not dead, but he talks to the family as if she is.

One person reads aloud Friar Lawrence's lines 65–83. Pause frequently. In each pause, the other person says aloud what the Friar is really thinking at that moment.

## 2 'Black funeral'

You will need an empty space for this activity.

Capulet's lines 84–90 have a rhythm all of their own. Walk around the room reading the lines aloud. Every time you come to a 'turning' word such as 'turn', or 'to', change direction in your walking. Invent different ways of physically expressing the movement of his speech. Is there a natural way in which these lines should be spoken? You will find another activity based on Capulet's lines 84–90 (and Juliet's funeral) on page 168.

## 3 The ballad of Juliet

Make up a ballad telling the story of Juliet in Act 4. You might use one of the musicians' songs in Scene 5 as a title.

---

**rosemary** a herb associated with funerals (and weddings)
**office** proper purposes
**corse** corpse
**dirges** sad songs

**low'r** lour, frown
**by my troth** in truth
**dump** sad tune (so 'merry dump' is yet another oxymoron – see page 212)

> The most you sought was her promotion,
> For 'twas your heaven she should be advanced,
> And weep ye now, seeing she is advanced
> Above the clouds, as high as heaven itself?
> O, in this love, you love your child so ill                     75
> That you run mad, seeing that she is well.
> She's not well married that lives married long,
> But she's best married that dies married young.
> Dry up your tears, and stick your rosemary
> On this fair corse, and as the custom is,                       80
> And in her best array, bear her to church;
> For though fond nature bids us all lament,
> Yet nature's tears are reason's merriment.

CAPULET All things that we ordainèd festival,
> Turn from their office to black funeral:                        85
> Our instruments to melancholy bells,
> Our wedding cheer to a sad burial feast;
> Our solemn hymns to sullen dirges change;
> Our bridal flowers serve for a buried corse;
> And all things change them to the contrary.                     90

FRIAR LAWRENCE Sir, go you in, and, madam, go with him,
> And go, Sir Paris. Every one prepare
> To follow this fair corse unto her grave.
> The heavens do low'r upon you for some ill;
> Move them no more by crossing their high will.                  95

> *[They all, but the Nurse and the Musicians, go forth,*
> *casting rosemary on her, and shutting the curtains]*

FIRST MUSICIAN Faith, we may put up our pipes and be gone.

NURSE Honest good fellows, ah put up, put up,
> For well you know this is a pitiful case.                    *[Exit]*

FIRST MUSICIAN Ay, by my troth, the case may be amended.

*Enter* PETER.

PETER Musicians, O musicians, 'Heart's ease', 'Heart's ease'! O,   100
> and you will have me live, play 'Heart's ease'.

FIRST MUSICIAN Why 'Heart's ease'?

PETER O musicians, because my heart itself plays 'My heart is full'.
> O play me some merry dump to comfort me.

*Peter talks with the musicians. They do not care for his humour.*

### 1 Staging the musicians (in groups of four)

Each person takes a part (Peter, musicians). Read through lines 100–38. Work out how you would stage them. Would the scene work if you changed the musicians into modern rock or pop stars?

### 2 To cut or not to cut? (in groups of four)

What's the purpose of this scene of the musicians?

Sometimes these lines (100–38) are cut from performances. Talk together about whether you would cut the musicians and Peter from your production. Two argue for leaving out this part of the play. Two argue against cutting. Share your verdict and reasons with the rest of the class.

### 3 Improvise (in groups of three)

Improvise the story the three musicians tell their friends. They have been hired to play at the wedding of Juliet and Paris. But unexpected things happen . . .

### 4 Make up a popular song (in pairs)

Can you put Peter's three lines 'When griping griefs the heart doth wound . . . her silver sound' (lines 120–2) to your own music? Raps or chants will do nicely!

In lines 100–04 you will find the titles of two popular songs of Shakespeare's day: 'Heart's ease' and 'My heart is full'. Their words are now lost. Make up a song using one or both titles.

the gleek an insult. Today Peter would probably accompany his words with a two-fingered gesture!
the minstrel good-for-nothing (Peter further insults the musicians)

Catling, Rebeck, Soundpost Peter calls the musicians by the names of parts of their instruments. Do you think these are their actual names or is Peter once more insulting them?

MUSICIANS Not a dump we, 'tis no time to play now.                         105
PETER You will not then?
FIRST MUSICIAN No.
PETER I will then give it you soundly.
FIRST MUSICIAN What will you give us?
PETER No money, on my faith, but the gleek; I will give you the     110
    minstrel.
FIRST MUSICIAN Then will I give you the serving-creature.
PETER Then will I lay the serving-creature's dagger on your pate. I will
    carry no crotchets, I'll re you, I'll fa you. Do you note me?
FIRST MUSICIAN And you re us and fa us, you note us.                    115
SECOND MUSICIAN Pray you put up your dagger, and put out your
    wit.
PETER Then have at you with my wit! I will dry-beat you with an iron
    wit, and put up my iron dagger. Answer me like men:
        'When griping griefs the heart doth wound,              120
        And doleful dumps the mind oppress,
        Then music with her silver sound –'
    Why 'silver sound'? why 'music with her silver sound'? What say
    you, Simon Catling?
FIRST MUSICIAN Marry, sir, because silver hath a sweet sound.          125
PETER Prates! What say you, Hugh Rebeck?
SECOND MUSICIAN I say 'silver sound' because musicians sound for
    silver.
PETER Prates too! What say you, James Soundpost?
THIRD MUSICIAN Faith, I know not what to say.                          130
PETER O, I cry you mercy, you are the singer; I will say for you: It
    is 'music with her silver sound' because musicians have no gold
    for sounding.
        'Then music with her silver sound
        With speedy help doth lend redress.'              *Exit*   135
FIRST MUSICIAN What a pestilent knave is this same!
SECOND MUSICIAN Hang him, Jack! Come, we'll in here, tarry for the
    mourners, and stay dinner.
                                                   *Exeunt*

# Looking back at Act 4
*Activities for groups or individuals*

## 1 Juliet's funeral

'Every one prepare
To follow this corse unto her grave'

In the eighteenth and nineteenth centuries, theatre productions often added a scene to show the funeral of Juliet. The playbill opposite advertises a production at Drury Lane in 1756.

In groups of eight to twelve work out how you will show Juliet's funeral. Use Capulet's lines 84–90 from Scene 5. Make your presentation as dramatically striking as possible. You could speak or sing or chant the words. Each group member could choose to be a character and use some of that character's mourning language (lines 34–64 in Scene 5) in the funeral march.

You may be able to find some music to accompany your group's actions, such as 'The Dead March', from Handel's *Saul*, or Fauré's *Requiem*.

## 2 What else was added?

Study the playbill opposite to find out what else David Garrick added in 1756 to Shakespeare's *Romeo and Juliet*.

## 3 Design a poster

Theatre posters advertising plays have changed greatly since the playbill shown opposite. Collect some examples of recent posters or advertisements for plays. Design your own poster for a production of *Romeo and Juliet*.

## 4 Romeo's absence

Shakespeare keeps Romeo off-stage throughout this act. Talk together about some of the reasons for his absence.

## 5 Telling lies – is it always wrong?

Juliet deceives her father in Scene 2. Talk together about whether you think it's right to lie to your parents. When might you deceive your parents?

AT THE

# TheatreRoyal in *Drury-Lane*,

This prefent *Tuefday*, being the 16th of *November*, 1756
Will be prefented a PLAY, call'd

# RO MEO and *JULIET*.

## Romeo by Mr. GARRICK,

*Efcalus* by Mr. B R A N S B Y,

## Capulet by Mr. BERRY,

*Paris* by Mr. J E F F E R S O N,
*Benvolio* by Mr. U S H E R,
*Mountague* by Mr. B U R T O N,
*Tibalt* by Mr. B L A K E S,

# Fryar *Lawrence* by Mr. HAVARD,

# *Mercutio* by Mr. WOODWARD,

# Lady *Capulet* by Mrs. PRITCHARD,

# *Nurfe* by Mrs. M A C K L I N,

# *Juliet* by Mifs PRITCHARD.

With the A D D I T I O N A L S C E N E Reprefenting

# The Funeral PROCESSION

# To the MONUMENT of the *CAPULETS*.

The V O C A L P A R T S by
Mr. *Beard*, Mr. *Champnefs* and *Others*.
In Act I. a *Mafquerade Dance* proper to the Play.
To which will be added a F A R C E, call'd

# The A N A T O M I S T.

Monf. *Le Medecin* by Mr. B L A K E S,
*Crifpin* by Mr. Y A T E S,
*Beatrice* by Mrs. B E N N E T.

Boxes 5s. Pit 3s. Firft Gallery 2s. Upper Gallery 1s.
Places for the Boxes to be had of Mr. V A R N E Y, at the Stage-
door of the *Theatre*.
† *No Perfons to be admitted behind the Scenes, nor any Money to be returned
after the* Curtain *is drawn up*. *Vivat* R E X.

To-morrow, the MOURNING BRIDE. *Ofmyn* by Mr. MOSSOP,
(*Being the Firft Time of his appearing in that Character.*)

*Romeo, in Mantua, talks joyfully of his strange dream. But Balthasar brings him dreadful news.*

## 1 Romeo's dream – fill in the details (in groups of four)

Romeo tells only the bare outline of his dream (lines 6–9). He gives none of the details. Talk together about some of the possible details of his dream and about possible interpretations of the dream.

Work out a mime or short play showing Romeo's dream.

## 2 Balthasar's predicament – how to tell Romeo (in groups of three)

Imagine you are Balthasar, riding from Verona to Mantua to tell Romeo of Juliet's death. What are your thoughts as you ride – just how are you to tell Romeo the dreadful news? Work through different ways you might recount the story, and your fears about each.

## 3 Mantua – a change of scene

The previous scene is set in Juliet's bedroom in Verona. Act 5 begins in Mantua, twenty-five miles away. Work out how you would carry out the scene change swiftly and effectively. Use the Elizabethan stage on page 214, or the stage set on page 217, or make up your own stage setting. Remember, the audience must clearly recognise the shift in location. Also remember that the location suggested here ('A street in Mantua') has been made up for this edition (see page 4, Activity 4). Shakespeare certainly places Romeo in Mantua, but he leaves it to your imagination to work out how the location will be shown on stage.

---

**presage** foretell, promise
**bosom's lord** heart (or love?)
**booted** in riding boots

**presently took post** immediately rode here on horseback
**office** duty

# ACT 5   SCENE 1
## A street in Mantua

*Enter* ROMEO.

ROMEO  If I may trust the flattering truth of sleep,
My dreams presage some joyful news at hand.
My bosom's lord sits lightly in his throne,
And all this day an unaccustomed spirit
Lifts me above the ground with cheerful thoughts.          5
I dreamt my lady came and found me dead
(Strange dream that gives a dead man leave to think!),
And breathed such life with kisses in my lips
That I revived and was an emperor.
Ah me, how sweet is love itself possessed,          10
When but love's shadows are so rich in joy!

*Enter Romeo's man* [BALTHASAR, *booted*].

News from Verona! How now, Balthasar?
Dost thou not bring me letters from the Friar?
How doth my lady? Is my father well?
How doth my Juliet? That I ask again,          15
For nothing can be ill if she be well.
BALTHASAR  Then she is well and nothing can be ill:
Her body sleeps in Capels' monument,
And her immortal part with angels lives.
I saw her laid low in her kindred's vault,          20
And presently took post to tell it you.
O pardon me for bringing these ill news,
Since you did leave it for my office, sir.

*Dismissing Balthasar to hire horses, Romeo resolves to kill himself that night in the tomb with Juliet. But how? The apothecary who sells poisons comes into his mind.*

## 1 'Then I defy you, stars!' (in pairs)

What advice would you give to an actor playing Romeo as to how he could deliver line 24? If the actor asked you what is in Romeo's mind at this moment what would you say? There's something to help you on page 204.

## 2 Is Romeo brave or foolish or . . .? (in small groups)

'Well, Juliet, I will lie with thee tonight' (line 34)

Romeo resolves to kill himself that night in Capulet's monument. Talk together about whether you think this is a brave decision. How else can it be seen? Does Romeo really have any alternative?

## 3 The apothecary and his shop

Lines 37–48 give a detailed description of the apothecary and his shop. Make an imaginative drawing including as much of Shakespeare's description as you can. As you draw, think why such a precise description is given at this point in the play.

## 4 Early closing in Mantua?

The apothecary's shop is shut. Apparently it's a holiday in Mantua. One production in the late 1980s made a great show of the holiday festivities going on in Mantua. They were presented as a carnival, with much political protest added (actors wore huge heads of contemporary politicians).

If you were directing the play, would you show the 'holiday' in some way? Argue for or against the suitability of presenting the holiday on stage. How do your views add to audience response at this point?

**import** suggest
**apothecary** druggist, someone who sells ingredients for medicine
**weeds** clothes

**culling of simples** picking herbs to use in medicines
**beggarly account** poor number
**caitiff** miserable, pitiable

ROMEO Is it e'en so? then I defy you, stars!
   Thou knowest my lodging, get me ink and paper,    25
   And hire post-horses; I will hence tonight.
BALTHASAR I do beseech you, sir, have patience:
   Your looks are pale and wild, and do import
   Some misadventure.
ROMEO       Tush, thou art deceived.
   Leave me, and do the thing I bid thee do.     30
   Hast thou no letters to me from the Friar?
BALTHASAR No, my good lord.
ROMEO       No matter, get thee gone,
   And hire those horses; I'll be with thee straight.
               *Exit* [*Balthasar*]
   Well, Juliet, I will lie with thee tonight.
   Let's see for means. O mischief, thou art swift   35
   To enter in the thoughts of desperate men!
   I do remember an apothecary,
   And hereabouts 'a dwells, which late I noted
   In tattered weeds, with overwhelming brows,
   Culling of simples; meagre were his looks,    40
   Sharp misery had worn him to the bones;
   And in his needy shop a tortoise hung,
   An alligator stuffed, and other skins
   Of ill-shaped fishes, and about his shelves
   A beggarly account of empty boxes,      45
   Green earthen pots, bladders, and musty seeds,
   Remnants of packthread, and old cakes of roses
   Were thinly scattered, to make up a show.
   Noting this penury, to myself I said,
   'And if a man did need a poison now,     50
   Whose sale is present death in Mantua,
   Here lives a caitiff wretch would sell it him.'
   O this same thought did but forerun my need,
   And this same needy man must sell it me.
   As I remember, this should be the house.    55
   Being holiday, the beggar's shop is shut.
   What ho, apothecary!

*The penniless apothecary sells poison to Romeo even though he knows the penalty for doing so is death. Romeo leaves for Verona and Juliet's tomb, determined to drink the poison there.*

## 1 Act out Romeo's meeting with the apothecary (in pairs)

First read through lines 57–86, each partner taking a role. Then talk about how you might stage the action. Think carefully about the state of mind of each character at this moment. Can you show those states of mind in your presentation?

What does the apothecary look like? In *Nicholas Nickleby*, Charles Dickens wrote about a performance of *Romeo and Juliet*. The artist Phiz drew Nicholas and Smike as Romeo and the apothecary. Smike had terrible problems learning his lines!

**ducats** gold coins
**dram** dose

**soon-speeding gear** quick-acting poison
**trunk** body

[*Enter* APOTHECARY.]

APOTHECARY                Who calls so loud?
ROMEO  Come hither, man. I see that thou art poor.
          Hold, there is forty ducats; let me have
          A dram of poison, such soon-speeding gear          60
          As will disperse itself through all the veins,
          That the life-weary taker may fall dead,
          And that the trunk may be discharged of breath
          As violently as hasty powder fired
          Doth hurry from the fatal cannon's womb.           65
APOTHECARY  Such mortal drugs I have, but Mantua's law
          Is death to any he that utters them.
ROMEO  Art thou so bare and full of wretchedness,
          And fearest to die? Famine is in thy cheeks,
          Need and oppression starveth in thy eyes,          70
          Contempt and beggary hangs upon thy back;
          The world is not thy friend, nor the world's law,
          The world affords no law to make thee rich;
          Then be not poor, but break it and take this.
APOTHECARY  My poverty, but not my will, consents.          75
ROMEO  I pay thy poverty and not thy will.
APOTHECARY  Put this in any liquid thing you will
          And drink it off, and if you had the strength
          Of twenty men, it would dispatch you straight.
ROMEO  There is thy gold, worse poison to men's souls,      80
          Doing more murder in this loathsome world,
          Than these poor compounds that thou mayst not sell.
          I sell thee poison, thou hast sold me none.
          Farewell, buy food, and get thyself in flesh.
                                        [*Exit Apothecary*]
          Come, cordial and not poison, go with me           85
          To Juliet's grave, for there must I use thee.      *Exit*

*Friar John tells how an unlucky mischance prevented him delivering Friar Lawrence's letter to Romeo. Friar Lawrence determines to break into Capulet's monument to be with Juliet when she awakes.*

## 1 'Unhappy fortune!' – Friar John's delay

Friar John explains that he was seeking another Franciscan friar to accompany him to Mantua in order to deliver Friar Lawrence's letter to Romeo. He found his brother friar visiting the sick. There disaster struck! The 'searchers' called!

The 'searchers' were health officers of the town appointed to prevent the spread of disease by examining dead bodies to establish the cause of death. They thought that the Franciscans were in a house where plague raged, so refused to allow them to travel ('sealed up the doors'). This was common practice in London at the time Shakespeare was writing.

**a Echo!**
Read lines 5–12 aloud but add 'unhappy fortune!' after every punctuation mark.

**b Improvise!** (in groups of five or six)
Two of the group take the roles of Friar John and his fellow monk. The others are the 'searchers' who refuse them permission to leave the house. Improvise what took place as the searchers refuse to grant the Friars' pleading to be allowed out to travel to Mantua.

**c Act out the scene** (in pairs)
Take the roles of Friar Lawrence and Friar John. Before you read through the scene, the person who is Friar John should do ten quick press-ups (or quickly step up and down on a chair twenty times) to become breathless. Now, read through the scene as quickly as you can. Change roles and repeat the exercise. Does becoming breathless help in speaking Friar John's lines?

---

**barefoot brother** Franciscan friar
**associate** accompany (Franciscans nearly always travelled in pairs – can you think why?)

**bare** carried
**nice** trivial
**crow** crowbar
**beshrew** blame
**corse** corpse

## ACT 5   SCENE 2
## Friar Lawrence's cell

*Enter* FRIAR JOHN.

FRIAR JOHN  Holy Franciscan Friar, brother, ho!

*Enter* [FRIAR] LAWRENCE.

FRIAR LAWRENCE  This same should be the voice of Friar John.
Welcome from Mantua. What says Romeo?
Or if his mind be writ, give me his letter.
FRIAR JOHN  Going to find a barefoot brother out,                    5
One of our order, to associate me,
Here in this city visiting the sick,
And finding him, the searchers of the town,
Suspecting that we both were in a house
Where the infectious pestilence did reign,                           10
Sealed up the doors, and would not let us forth,
So that my speed to Mantua there was stayed.
FRIAR LAWRENCE  Who bare my letter then to Romeo?
FRIAR JOHN  I could not send it – here it is again –
Nor get a messenger to bring it thee,                                15
So fearful were they of infection.
FRIAR LAWRENCE  Unhappy fortune! By my brotherhood,
The letter was not nice but full of charge,
Of dear import, and the neglecting it
May do much danger. Friar John, go hence,                           20
Get me an iron crow and bring it straight
Unto my cell.
FRIAR JOHN  Brother, I'll go and bring it thee.                *Exit*
FRIAR LAWRENCE  Now must I to the monument alone,
Within this three hours will fair Juliet wake.                       25
She will beshrew me much that Romeo
Hath had no notice of these accidents;
But I will write again to Mantua,
And keep her at my cell till Romeo come,
Poor living corse, closed in a dead man's tomb!        *Exit*    30

*Paris visits Juliet's tomb to lay flowers and mourn. His page whistles to warn him someone is coming.*

## 1 Masters and servants (in pairs)

Face each other, and as one reads each section of Paris' lines 1–9, the other mimes each action.

Then repeat, but this time speak only the words of command ('give', 'hence', etc.). How many orders does Paris give to his page?

## 2 Night and churchyards (in small groups)

Shakespeare uses words to create time, place and atmosphere. Sharing the lines between you, read everything on the opposite page. Emphasise each word that helps create night-time and graveyards. For example, your first emphasised word is 'torch'.

Follow this by reading aloud each of the words you emphasised. After each word add your own comment as to how it creates an atmosphere of time ('night'), or place ('churchyard').

## 3 Paris' six lines of mourning – something to think about

Read lines 12–17. Do you find them artificial and formal, or do they seem to come from Paris' heart? It's helpful to compare them with Romeo's own mourning at lines 85–120 on pages 183–5.

stand aloof go some distance away
canopy the stone covering of the tomb (instead of the fabric covering Juliet's bed)

sweet water perfumed water
obsequies funeral rites

# ACT 5   SCENE 3
## A churchyard, outside the tomb of the Capulets

*Enter* PARIS *and his* PAGE [*with flowers and sweet water and a torch*].

PARIS  Give me thy torch, boy. Hence, and stand aloof.
      Yet put it out, for I would not be seen.
      Under yond yew trees lay thee all along,
      Holding thy ear close to the hollow ground,
      So shall no foot upon the churchyard tread,      5
      Being loose, unfirm with digging up of graves,
      But thou shalt hear it. Whistle then to me
      As signal that thou hear'st something approach.
      Give me those flowers. Do as I bid thee, go.
PAGE  [*Aside*] I am almost afraid to stand alone      10
      Here in the churchyard, yet I will adventure.      [*Retires*]
           [*Paris strews the tomb with flowers.*]
PARIS  Sweet flower, with flowers thy bridal bed I strew –
      O woe, thy canopy is dust and stones! –
      Which with sweet water nightly I will dew,
      Or wanting that, with tears distilled by moans.      15
      The obsequies that I for thee will keep
      Nightly shall be to strew thy grave and weep.
           *Whistle Boy.*
      The boy gives warning, something doth approach.
      What cursèd foot wanders this way tonight,
      To cross my obsequies and true love's rite?      20
      What, with a torch? Muffle me, night, a while.      [*Retires*]

*Romeo, determined to force open the tomb, dismisses Balthasar on pain of death. Balthasar resolves to stay and watch. As Romeo begins to force entry, Paris steps forward to challenge him.*

## 1 Masters and servants (in pairs)

Take Romeo's lines 22–42 and carry out a similar activity to that on page 178. One person reads, the other mimes every action and echoes each word of command or words that are threatening.

Afterwards divide the lines into four sections: 22–7, 28–32, 33–9, 40–2. Talk together about how each section shows you a different aspect of Romeo's feelings and personality.

## 2 Why does Romeo lie? (in groups of four)

Why does Romeo tell a lie (or two lies) to Balthasar in lines 28–32? Remember, there's no 'right' answer to this, so explore explanations that seem possible in the light of all you know about Romeo.

## 3 Death takes a meal (in groups of five to eight)

In lines 45–8, Romeo compares the tomb with Death eating human beings (Juliet is 'the dearest morsel'). Make a tableau of one of these four lines to show this image as vividly as you can.

## 4 Balthasar decides to stay and watch

If you were Balthasar, would you stay to watch after Romeo has threatened you so drastically?

---

**mattock** a kind of pickaxe
**wrenching iron** crowbar

**jealous** suspicious
**maw** stomach

*Enter* ROMEO *and* [BALTHASAR *with a torch, a mattock, and a crow of iron*].

ROMEO  Give me that mattock and the wrenching iron.
       Hold, take this letter; early in the morning
       See thou deliver it to my lord and father.
       Give me the light. Upon thy life I charge thee,                25
       What e'er thou hear'st or seest, stand all aloof,
       And do not interrupt me in my course.
       Why I descend into this bed of death
       Is partly to behold my lady's face,
       But chiefly to take thence from her dead finger               30
       A precious ring, a ring that I must use
       In dear employment; therefore hence, be gone.
       But if thou, jealous, dost return to pry
       In what I farther shall intend to do,
       By heaven, I will tear thee joint by joint,                   35
       And strew this hungry churchyard with thy limbs.
       The time and my intents are savage-wild,
       More fierce and more inexorable far
       Than empty tigers or the roaring sea.
BALTHASAR  I will be gone, sir, and not trouble ye.              40
ROMEO  So shalt thou show me friendship. Take thou that,
                 [*Gives a purse.*]
       Live and be prosperous, and farewell, good fellow.
BALTHASAR  [*Aside*] For all this same, I'll hide me hereabout,
       His looks I fear, and his intents I doubt.          [*Retires*]
ROMEO  Thou detestable maw, thou womb of death,                  45
       Gorged with the dearest morsel of the earth,
       Thus I enforce thy rotten jaws to open,
       And in despite I'll cram thee with more food.
          [*Romeo begins to open the tomb.*]
PARIS  This is that banished haughty Montague,
       That murdered my love's cousin, with which grief             50
       It is supposèd the fair creature died,
       And here is come to do some villainous shame
       To the dead bodies. I will apprehend him.
           [*Steps forth.*]

*Paris tries to arrest Romeo, but is slain by him. Romeo, dismayed to find whom he has killed, resolves to grant Paris' dying wish, and lays his body beside Juliet's.*

### 1 Does the order matter? (in groups of three)

Read Paris' lines 54–7 to each other, but keep changing the order of these lines. Do you think anything is gained by changing the order of these lines? Talk together about why you think they should be in the order given.

### 2 Stage directions only (in groups of four)

Make a list of all the stage directions given so far in this scene. Use them to act out what's happened up to this point.

### 3 'Sour misfortune's book!' (line 82)

Who else in the play do you think would join Romeo and Paris in a book of people afflicted by unhappy mischance and accident? The character list on page 1 will help your choice.

Who might have a place in a modern book of sour misfortune?

### 4 Light in death – something to imagine

Let your imagination roam over Romeo's lines 83–6. What do you see in your mind's eye?

It may be helpful to know that in architecture a 'lantern' is a glass turret on the roof of a building. Its purpose is to let in light. A 'feasting presence' is a room in a palace where kings received and entertained visitors.

---

**unhallowed** unholy
**conjuration** appeal, entreaty
**Watch** police (but in Shakespeare's time there was no police force like today's. Instead, citizens (the Watch) patrolled the streets at night)

**betossèd** disturbed

        Stop thy unhallowed toil, vile Montague!
        Can vengeance be pursued further than death?     55
        Condemnèd villain, I do apprehend thee.
        Obey and go with me, for thou must die.
ROMEO I must indeed, and therefore came I hither.
        Good gentle youth, tempt not a desp'rate man,
        Fly hence and leave me. Think upon these gone,     60
        Let them affright thee. I beseech thee, youth,
        Put not another sin upon my head,
        By urging me to fury: O be gone!
        By heaven, I love thee better than myself,
        For I come hither armed against myself.     65
        Stay not, be gone; live, and hereafter say,
        A madman's mercy bid thee run away.
PARIS I do defy thy conjuration,
        And apprehend thee for a felon here.
ROMEO Wilt thou provoke me? then have at thee, boy!     70
                [*They fight.*]
PAGE O Lord, they fight! I will go call the Watch.     [*Exit*]
PARIS O, I am slain! [*Falls.*] If thou be merciful,
        Open the tomb, lay me with Juliet. [*Dies.*]
ROMEO In faith, I will. Let me peruse this face.
        Mercutio's kinsman, noble County Paris!     75
        What said my man, when my betossèd soul
        Did not attend him as we rode? I think
        He told me Paris should have married Juliet.
        Said he not so? or did I dream it so?
        Or am I mad, hearing him talk of Juliet,     80
        To think it was so? O give me thy hand,
        One writ with me in sour misfortune's book!
        I'll bury thee in a triumphant grave.
        A grave? O no, a lantern, slaughtered youth;
        For here lies Juliet, and her beauty makes     85
        This vault a feasting presence full of light.
        Death, lie thou there, by a dead man interred.
        [*Laying Paris in the tomb.*]

*Romeo gazes on Juliet and, determined to join her in death, drinks the poison.*

## 1 Romeo's last words (in pairs or individually)

These are the last words Romeo speaks in the play. Read the lines through several times, speaking them in different ways. If you choose to work with a partner, share the lines between you. Pick out the lines or phrases that have most appeal for you. How could you express those lines or phrases in ways that you would find imaginatively satisfying?

## 2 Direct Romeo (in pairs)

Imagine that the actor playing Romeo has asked you for advice on how to speak and play this final speech. Work out the notes you would give him. Identify the different sections of the speech and the actions you think should accompany them.

One way of dividing up the speech could be: lines 88–91, lines 91–6, lines 97–101, lines 101–5, lines 106–12, lines 112–18, lines 119–20. Prepare notes for each of these sections, suggesting meanings and possible actions.

## 3 Share the speech (in a large group – up to thirty)

Divide the speech up between the whole group. Each person takes a line or more and learns their words.

Work out the most dramatic way of presenting the speech as a group performance. Use whatever space you have to gain greater effect.

---

**keepers** gaolers, prison warders
**ensign** flag
**paramour** lover
**set up . . . rest** make my full, final commitment (an image from a card game)

**engrossing** all-owning ('seal' and 'bargain' echo Romeo's legal imagery of an everlasting contract with Death)
**conduct** i.e. the poison (but notice that 'conduct', 'guide', 'pilot', 'bark' (ship), all emphasise Romeo's image of life as a sea-journey ending in disaster)

How oft when men are at the point of death
Have they been merry, which their keepers call
A light'ning before death! O how may I                              90
Call this a light'ning? O my love, my wife,
Death, that hath sucked the honey of thy breath,
Hath had no power yet upon thy beauty:
Thou art not conquered, beauty's ensign yet
Is crimson in thy lips and in thy cheeks,                           95
And Death's pale flag is not advancèd there.
Tybalt, liest thou there in thy bloody sheet?
O, what more favour can I do to thee
Than with that hand that cut thy youth in twain
To sunder his that was thine enemy?                                 100
Forgive me, cousin. Ah, dear Juliet,
Why art thou yet so fair? Shall I believe
That unsubstantial Death is amorous,
And that the lean abhorrèd monster keeps
Thee here in dark to be his paramour?                               105
For fear of that, I still will stay with thee,
And never from this palace of dim night
Depart again. Here, here will I remain
With worms that are thy chambermaids; O here
Will I set up my everlasting rest,                                  110
And shake the yoke of inauspicious stars
From this world-wearied flesh. Eyes, look your last!
Arms, take your last embrace! and, lips, O you
The doors of breath, seal with a righteous kiss
A dateless bargain to engrossing Death!                            115
Come, bitter conduct, come, unsavoury guide!
Thou desperate pilot, now at once run on
The dashing rocks thy seasick weary bark!
Here's to my love! [*Drinks.*] O true apothecary!
Thy drugs are quick. Thus with a kiss I die. [*Dies.*]             120

*Balthasar tells Friar Lawrence that Romeo is in the tomb. Entering the vault, the Friar finds the dead Romeo and Paris. Juliet begins to awaken.*

## 1 Urgency and fear in the Friar's words (in pairs)

Take each line the Friar says on the opposite page, but say aloud only the words that build up an atmosphere of urgency and fear.

You may find it helpful to know that if someone 'stumbled', it would be considered by Elizabethans to be an ill-omen (if you 'stumbled', things would begin to go wrong).

## 2 How to speak the lines? (in pairs)

Take the roles of Friar Lawrence and Balthasar. Read all the opposite page aloud.

How should lines 129–31 be spoken? These are shared between Friar Lawrence and Balthasar. There's a theatrical convention that when a line is shared, there should be no pauses between the speakers. From your own experience of speaking the words, do you agree?

## 3 Balthasar's puzzling words (in groups of three)

Balthasar has such a small part that he is often overlooked in theatre productions. Yet he says some curious things to the Friar. Talk together to find what you think about them:

- 'one that knows you well' – but does he? Friar Lawrence does not seem to know he's Romeo's servant at line 129
- 'half an hour' – does that seem likely?
- why does Balthasar say he dreamed of Romeo and Paris fighting?

Remember: there's no 'right' answer to these puzzles. Talk together about possibilities that you think are dramatically and imaginatively satisfying.

**unthrifty** unfortunate

*Enter* FRIAR [LAWRENCE] *with lantern, crow, and spade.*

FRIAR LAWRENCE Saint Francis be my speed! how oft tonight
    Have my old feet stumbled at graves! Who's there?
BALTHASAR Here's one, a friend, and one that knows you well.
FRIAR LAWRENCE Bliss be upon you! Tell me, good my friend,
    What torch is yond that vainly lends his light       125
    To grubs and eyeless skulls? As I discern,
    It burneth in the Capels' monument.
BALTHASAR It doth so, holy sir, and there's my master,
    One that you love.
FRIAR LAWRENCE           Who is it?
BALTHASAR                Romeo.
FRIAR LAWRENCE How long hath he been there?
BALTHASAR                Full half an hour.   130
FRIAR LAWRENCE Go with me to the vault.
BALTHASAR                I dare not, sir.
    My master knows not but I am gone hence,
    And fearfully did menace me with death
    If I did stay to look on his intents.
FRIAR LAWRENCE Stay then, I'll go alone. Fear comes upon me.   135
    O, much I fear some ill unthrifty thing.
BALTHASAR As I did sleep under this yew tree here,
    I dreamt my master and another fought,
    And that my master slew him.        [*Retires*]
FRIAR LAWRENCE            Romeo!
    [*Friar stoops and looks on the blood and weapons.*]
    Alack, alack, what blood is this which stains   140
    The stony entrance of this sepulchre?
    What mean these masterless and gory swords
    To lie discoloured by this place of peace?
              [*Enters the tomb.*]
    Romeo! O, pale! Who else? What, Paris too?
    And steeped in blood? Ah, what an unkind hour   145
    Is guilty of this lamentable chance!
              [*Juliet rises.*]
    The lady stirs.

*Friar Lawrence, fearful of discovery, leaves the tomb, begging Juliet to go with him. She refuses, and stabs herself because she prefers to join Romeo in death. The Watch enter.*

---

### 1 Friar Lawrence's fears (in groups of three or four)

Read lines 151–9 to each other, each person speaking a sentence then handing on. Repeat several times, a different person beginning each reading.

Talk about what these lines tell you about the Friar at this moment; his state of mind, his motives, and his feelings for Juliet. You might also try reading his eight sentences in a quite different order from Shakespeare's to see what difference such a jumbled-up reading makes.

### 2 Juliet's death (in pairs)

Why did Shakespeare give Juliet a much shorter 'death speech' than Romeo? Show how you would stage her final words convincingly.

### 3 'Rust' or 'rest'?

No one really knows whether Shakespeare wrote 'rust' or 'rest' at line 170. Which word do you think is most appropriate and why?

### 4 Where should the play end?

In the nineteenth century, productions often ended with the death of Juliet at line 170. Talk together about what you think a production of the play would gain and lose from ending at this point.

---

**churl** brute (but how do you think Juliet says the word?)
**haply** maybe

**restorative** medicine (the kiss will 'cure' her of life and restore her to Romeo)
**attach** arrest

JULIET  O comfortable Friar, where is my lord?
    I do remember well where I should be;
    And there I am. Where is my Romeo?         150
        *[Noise within.]*
FRIAR LAWRENCE  I hear some noise, lady. Come from that nest
    Of death, contagion, and unnatural sleep.
    A greater power than we can contradict
    Hath thwarted our intents. Come, come away.
    Thy husband in thy bosom there lies dead;       155
    And Paris too. Come, I'll dispose of thee
    Among a sisterhood of holy nuns.
    Stay not to question, for the Watch is coming.
    Come go, good Juliet, I dare no longer stay.     *Exit*
JULIET  Go get thee hence, for I will not away.        160
    What's here? a cup closed in my true love's hand?
    Poison I see hath been his timeless end.
    O churl, drunk all, and left no friendly drop
    To help me after? I will kiss thy lips,
    Haply some poison yet doth hang on them,       165
    To make me die with a restorative.
    Thy lips are warm.
CAPTAIN OF THE WATCH  *[Within]* Lead, boy, which way?
JULIET  Yea, noise? Then I'll be brief. O happy dagger,
        *[Taking Romeo's dagger.]*
    This is thy sheath;
        *[Stabs herself.]*
        there rust, and let me die.       170
    *[Falls on Romeo's body and dies.]*

    *Enter [Paris's] Boy and* WATCH.

PAGE  This is the place, there where the torch doth burn.
CAPTAIN OF THE WATCH
    The ground is bloody, search about the churchyard.
    Go, some of you, whoe'er you find attach.
        *[Exeunt some of the Watch]*
    *[The Captain enters the tomb and returns.]*
    Pitiful sight! here lies the County slain,
    And Juliet bleeding, warm, and newly dead,      175
    Who here hath lain this two days burièd.

*Balthasar and the Friar are arrested by the Watch. The Prince and the Capulets enter. The Captain tells what he knows.*

---

## 1 The Captain (in groups of four)

For a brief time, the Captain takes command of the stage. Look at all the lines he speaks (from line 168 on page 189 to line 201 opposite). Talk together about whether you think an actor should attempt to give him a distinct personality, or whether he should be simply an anonymous officer who makes no personal impact on the audience.

## 2 The Prince

Look back at the two other occasions when the Prince has appeared (1.1.72 and 3.1.132). What do the occasions have in common?

Think about the Prince's name: Escales. How does it signify that he is the 'top man' in Verona?

---

**ground** Even the Captain cannot resist a pun. His first 'ground' means 'earth', his second 'ground' means 'reason'

**circumstance** information
**descry** perceive, understand

Go tell the Prince, run to the Capulets,
Raise up the Montagues; some others search.
                    [*Exeunt others of the Watch*]
We see the ground whereon these woes do lie,
But the true ground of all these piteous woes                    180
We cannot without circumstance descry.

*Enter [one of the Watch with] Romeo's man [Balthasar].*

SECOND WATCHMAN
    Here's Romeo's man, we found him in the churchyard.
CAPTAIN OF THE WATCH
    Hold him in safety till the Prince come hither.

*Enter Friar [Lawrence] and another Watchman.*

THIRD WATCHMAN Here is a friar that trembles, sighs, and weeps.
    We took this mattock and this spade from him,                    185
    As he was coming from this churchyard's side.
CAPTAIN OF THE WATCH A great suspicion. Stay the friar too.

*Enter the* PRINCE [*with others*].

PRINCE What misadventure is so early up,
    That calls our person from our morning rest?

*Enter Capels* [CAPULET, LADY CAPULET].

CAPULET What should it be that is so shrieked abroad?                    190
LADY CAPULET O, the people in the street cry 'Romeo',
    Some 'Juliet', and some 'Paris', and all run
    With open outcry toward our monument.
PRINCE What fear is this which startles in your ears?
CAPTAIN OF THE WATCH
    Sovereign, here lies the County Paris slain,                    195
    And Romeo dead, and Juliet, dead before,
    Warm and new killed.
PRINCE Search, seek, and know how this foul murder comes.
CAPTAIN OF THE WATCH
    Here is a friar, and slaughtered Romeo's man,
    With instruments upon them, fit to open                    200
    These dead men's tombs.

*The Capulets and Montague enter the tomb to view their dead children.
At the Prince's command, Friar Lawrence begins to explain.*

---

## 1 Lady Montague's death

Montague announces that his wife is dead. This adds an extra layer of
poignancy to the play, but Shakespeare may have inserted it in order
to free the actor playing Lady Montague to take another part in this
scene. Remembering that she would have been played by a boy actor
in Shakespeare's time, which character (now on stage) do you think is
being 'doubled'?

## 2 The Prince – is he insensitive to Montague? (in pairs)

The Prince's three lines (lines 208–9, 213) seem very unsympathetic
towards Montague's feelings. Explore different ways of saying and
staging Prince Escales' lines. Try making him sympathetic to Montague. For example, might he offer a consoling hand? Then make him
hard and unfeeling.

## 3 Entering the tomb (in small groups)

The Capulets and Montague enter the tomb to see the dead bodies.
Work out, from the three stage directions opposite, how you would
stage those entries and returns from the tomb. What are the rest of
the cast to do whilst the parents are in the tomb? All the people on
stage should be involved in the action. Focus particularly on reactions
to lines 213–20.

## 4 A tableau of the death scene (in groups of ten or more)

Each group prepares a tableau to show just how every character is
behaving at the Prince's line 216 ('Seal . . .'). Hold the frozen
moment for thirty seconds. The spectators identify each character.
The illustrations on page 215 may help your imagination.

---

**hath mistane** has mistaken (is in
the wrong place)
**liege** lord

**press . . . grave** die before your
father
**impeach and purge** accuse and
find innocent

[*Capulet and Lady Capulet enter the tomb.*]
CAPULET  O heavens! O wife, look how our daughter bleeds!
            This dagger hath mistane, for lo his house
            Is empty on the back of Montague,
            And it mis-sheathèd in my daughter's bosom!              205
LADY CAPULET  O me, this sight of death is as a bell
            That warns my old age to a sepulchre.
                    [*They return from the tomb.*]

                    *Enter* MONTAGUE.

PRINCE  Come, Montague, for thou art early up
            To see thy son and heir now early down.
MONTAGUE  Alas, my liege, my wife is dead tonight;                   210
            Grief of my son's exile hath stopped her breath.
            What further woe conspires against mine age?
PRINCE  Look and thou shalt see.
                    [*Montague enters the tomb and returns.*]
MONTAGUE  O thou untaught! what manners is in this,
            To press before thy father to a grave?                   215
PRINCE  Seal up the mouth of outrage for a while,
            Till we can clear these ambiguities,
            And know their spring, their head, their true descent,
            And then will I be general of your woes,
            And lead you even to death. Mean time forbear,           220
            And let mischance be slave to patience.
            Bring forth the parties of suspicion.
FRIAR LAWRENCE  I am the greatest, able to do least,
            Yet most suspected, as the time and place
            Doth make against me, of this direful murder;            225
            And here I stand both to impeach and purge
            Myself condemnèd and myself excused.
PRINCE  Then say at once what thou dost know in this.
FRIAR LAWRENCE  I will be brief, for my short date of breath
            Is not so long as is a tedious tale.                     230
            Romeo, there dead, was husband to that Juliet,
            And she, there dead, that Romeo's faithful wife:

*Friar Lawrence tells his story to the Prince.*

---

## Friar Lawrence's explanation of events

Sometimes this long explanation is cut in productions of the play. Can you suggest why? It provides a valuable summary of events, even though it leaves out the Friar's reasons for acting as he did (to unite the families). The following activities will help you understand the story.

### 1 Point out who is involved (in groups of eight or more)

Each person takes a part (Friar, Romeo, Juliet, Tybalt, Paris, Friar John, the Nurse, Capulet). Stand in a circle. The Friar slowly reads the lines. Everyone points to whoever is mentioned, e.g. to the Friar on 'I'; to Romeo and Juliet on 'them' and 'their', and so on. You'll find it fun, and it will vividly remind you of the story. If you want a technical word for this pointing activity, it's 'deixis', pronounced deyesis or dakesis.

### 2 Act out the story (in groups of any size)

Act out the whole story, showing each action described (e.g. marriage, Tybalt's death, Romeo's banishment, etc.). The Friar packs in a tremendous amount of detail: there are at least thirty incidents to 'show'. Try to enact as many as possible.

An alternative is to divide up the different parts of the Friar's explanation. Each group takes a part of the tale to 'show'. For three groups, the sections could be lines 233–42; lines 243–52; lines 252–64.

### 3 The Friar's language

The Friar's language here is different from that of much of the rest of the play. It is direct, there are no puns, and coming from a priest it is surprisingly non-theological. How else would you describe Friar Lawrence's language here? Do you think it is typical of his usual language?

---

**perforce** by force
**privy** in the secret

**ought** anything
**miscarried** went wrong

I married them, and their stol'n marriage day
Was Tybalt's doomsday, whose untimely death
Banished the new-made bridegroom from this city,                    235
For whom, and not for Tybalt, Juliet pined.
You, to remove that siege of grief from her,
Betrothed and would have married her perforce
To County Paris. Then comes she to me,
And with wild looks bid me devise some mean                         240
To rid her from this second marriage,
Or in my cell there would she kill herself.
Then gave I her (so tutored by my art)
A sleeping potion, which so took effect
As I intended, for it wrought on her                               245
The form of death. Mean time I writ to Romeo
That he should hither come as this dire night
To help to take her from her borrowed grave,
Being the time the potion's force should cease.
But he which bore my letter, Friar John,                           250
Was stayed by accident, and yesternight
Returned my letter back. Then all alone,
At the prefixèd hour of her waking,
Came I to take her from her kindred's vault,
Meaning to keep her closely at my cell,                            255
Till I conveniently could send to Romeo.
But when I came, some minute ere the time
Of her awakening, here untimely lay
The noble Paris and true Romeo dead.
She wakes, and I entreated her come forth                          260
And bear this work of heaven with patience.
But then a noise did scare me from the tomb,
And she too desperate would not go with me,
But as it seems, did violence on herself.
All this I know, and to the marriage                               265
Her nurse is privy; and if ought in this
Miscarried by my fault, let my old life
Be sacrificed, some hour before his time,
Unto the rigour of severest law.

*Balthasar and Paris' page tell what they know. The Prince reads Romeo's letter, then calls Capulet and Montague to look on the deadly results of their quarrels.*

## 1  Act out the three stories (in groups of four to six)

Take the stories of Balthasar (lines 272–7), the Page (lines 281–5), and the Prince (lines 286–90). Act out as much detail as you can of one or more of the stories. You will find each story has at least six or seven 'scenes' that you can recreate.

## 2  Why include the stories? (in pairs)

Talk together about whether you think these stories add to the play, or could be safely cut from a production. What advice would you give to a director of the play as to whether they should be included or not?

## 3  Romeo's letter

What's in Romeo's letter to his father? The Prince reads a brief outline (lines 286–90). Write the full contents of the letter. Catch Romeo's state of mind at the moment he wrote it, shortly after hearing of Juliet's death.

## 4  'Heaven finds means to kill your joys with love' (in small groups)

Do you agree that 'heaven' has killed Romeo and Juliet? Or do you think the tragedy is caused by other reasons?

Pages 208–9 will help you explore why Romeo and Juliet died.

## 5  Make a time chart

The action of the play lasts from Sunday to Thursday. Draw a time chart, plotting every scene.

---

**in post** speedily (post-haste)
**for winking at your discords** for turning a blind eye to your quarrels
**kinsmen** Mercutio and Paris

PRINCE  We still have known thee for a holy man.                    270
        Where's Romeo's man? what can he say to this?
BALTHASAR  I brought my master news of Juliet's death,
        And then in post he came from Mantua
        To this same place, to this same monument.
        This letter he early bid me give his father,              275
        And threatened me with death, going in the vault,
        If I departed not and left him there.
PRINCE  Give me the letter, I will look on it.
        Where is the County's page that raised the Watch?
        Sirrah, what made your master in this place?            280
PAGE  He came with flowers to strew his lady's grave,
        And bid me stand aloof, and so I did.
        Anon comes one with light to ope the tomb,
        And by and by my master drew on him,
        And then I ran away to call the Watch.                   285
PRINCE  This letter doth make good the Friar's words,
        Their course of love, the tidings of her death;
        And here he writes that he did buy a poison
        Of a poor pothecary, and therewithal
        Came to this vault to die, and lie with Juliet.          290
        Where be these enemies? Capulet, Montague?
        See what a scourge is laid upon your hate,
        That heaven finds means to kill your joys with love!
        And I for winking at your discords too
        Have lost a brace of kinsmen. All are punished.          295

Romeo and Juliet

*Capulet and Montague make up their quarrel. They promise to set up a golden statue of Juliet and Romeo. The Prince closes the play.*

---

## 1 The golden statue of Romeo and Juliet (in small groups)

You have been commissioned to design the statue. Will it be like the effigies on Elizabethan tombs you can see in many churches, or some other design? Talk together about possibilities then prepare a tableau to show your statue. What inscription would you include at the base of the statue?

## 2 Pardoned and punished (a whole class activity)

Who is responsible for the tragedy? Arrange a trial of some of the major figures who you think might be accused of having a part in the deaths. Appoint a judge, prosecuting and defending counsels. The accused will be able to call witnesses if they wish. This activity will take time to prepare, so appoint a 'trial day' and do the necessary preparations.

## 3 What is the final stage picture? (in small groups)

Talk about the last image you wish the audience to see. An empty stage? If so, work out how you get everyone off, including the bodies.

Or you may want the audience to see a final tableau. What is it? Show the class your final moment of the play before the lights fade.

## 4 Show the whole play

Take the Prince's last six lines (lines 305–10) and the Prologue's fourteen lines (page 3). Put them together and work out actions which show the development of the whole play. A large group of ten or more with a narrator works well in this activity.

---

**jointure** marriage settlement (sum of money) made by the bridegroom's father to the bride. (All Capulet now asks from Montague is a handshake and reconciliation)

**Exeunt omnes** stage direction meaning everyone leaves the stage

CAPULET  O brother Montague, give me thy hand.
          This is my daughter's jointure, for no more
          Can I demand.
MONTAGUE              But I can give thee more,
          For I will raise her statue in pure gold,
          That whiles Verona by that name is known,                    300
          There shall no figure at such rate be set
          As that of true and faithful Juliet.
CAPULET  As rich shall Romeo's by his lady's lie,
          Poor sacrifices of our enmity!
PRINCE  A glooming peace this morning with it brings,                  305
          The sun for sorrow will not show his head.
          Go hence to have more talk of these sad things;
          Some shall be pardoned, and some punishèd:
          For never was a story of more woe
          Than this of Juliet and her Romeo.                           310
                                    [*Exeunt omnes*]

# Looking back at Act 5
*Activities for groups or individuals*

## 1 But is the feud really ended?

Do you think that a golden statue really marks the end of the bitter feud? Work in pairs. Experiment with Montague's and Capulet's lines at the end of the play (lines 296–304). Can the lines be spoken and acted in ways that show the quarrel will still continue?

## 2 Echoing images

Romeo's final speech (5.3.74–120) contains echoes of many of the images that have haunted the play. In groups of four to six, try this 'intercutting' exercise.

Collect lines from elsewhere in the play that echo lines in Romeo's last speech. Here are some examples if you need a start:

'sour misfortune's book' – see 1.3.82–93
'unsubstantial Death is amorous' – see 4.5.35–9
'inauspicious stars' – see Prologue line 6, 1.4.106–11, 3.5.54–7
'Here's to my love' – see 4.3.58
'O true apothecary' – see 5.1.59–65
'O my love . . . advanced there' – see 4.1.96–101
'Tybalt, liest thou there' – see 4.3.41–2 and 4.3.55–7

Make a dramatic presentation using the lines you have collected together with Romeo's last speech. One or two persons speak Romeo's lines 74–120, pausing frequently. In those pauses, the others echo lines taken from other parts of the play.

## 3 I died because . . .

Shakespeare seemed to have been fond of ghosts. He wrote some memorable ghost scenes. In *Richard III* all the dead come back in a dream to haunt King Richard.

Work in small groups. Make up a short play entitled 'Capulet's dream' (or 'nightmare'). It brings back all those who have died in the play. You might have each ghost telling why they died, and how they now feel about the feuding families. Don't be afraid to let your imagination run!

## 4  What the dickens!

The Royal Shakespeare Company mounted a memorable production of Charles Dickens' *Nicholas Nickleby*. In it there was a performance of the last scene of *Romeo and Juliet*. But the RSC turned it into a very happy ending!

Romeo and Juliet awoke to life. They hadn't really poisoned or stabbed themselves. Paris was similarly unharmed. Benvolio appeared to reveal he was really a girl, Benvolia! Paris instantly fell in love with her and proposed marriage! Only Tybalt wasn't granted a reprieve into life. Can you make up your own happy ending to the play?

## 5  How to play the Prince

In the RSC *Nicholas Nickleby* version of *Romeo and Juliet*, the Prince was very drunk – and very funny!

Experiment with different ways of playing the Prince: sober, drunk, angry, sad, maniacal . . .

## 6  The power of gold

Is Romeo's condemnation of gold (5.1.80–3) based on bitter personal experience? In small groups make up a mime or short play to show that money (gold) is the cause of the bloody quarrels between the Montagues and Capulets. If you want to see Shakespeare writing at full power in a condemnation of gold, see *Timon of Athens*.

## 7  Obituaries

You have been commissioned to write the obituaries of Romeo Montague and Juliet Capulet for the *Verona Herald* or some other newspaper of your choice. Talk together about what might be included in an obituary – then settle down to write.

## 8  Friar Lawrence writes his memoirs . . .

'It's ten years now since the deaths of Romeo and Juliet . . .'. What does the Friar think, looking back over this distance of time? What's he been doing since then? Imagine yourself as Friar Lawrence and complete your memoirs.

## 9  . . . and the Nurse is interviewed

Ten years later a newspaper reporter asks the Nurse for her account of what happened since she was last seen in the play . . .

# The story of Romeo and Juliet

There's no limit to the number of ways you can tell the story of Romeo and Juliet. You could write it in a single sentence:

'A boy and a girl, from families that hate each other bitterly, fall in love, but everything goes wrong for them and they kill themselves rather than be parted.'

Or you might write it in a paragraph, putting in more detail:

'The Montagues and Capulets are the two chief families of Verona. For years, they have been enemies in a bitter feud. Their teenage children, Romeo, a Montague, and Juliet, a Capulet, meet by accident at a grand party and fall instantly in love. They marry in secret, but cannot escape the consequences of their families' savage quarrel. Romeo's best friend Mercutio is killed by Tybalt of the Capulets. In revenge, Romeo kills Tybalt and is banished from Verona. Friar Lawrence devises dangerous plans to help Romeo and Juliet live together in happiness, but his schemes go terribly wrong. Romeo, believing Juliet is dead, kills himself to join her in death. Juliet finding Romeo dead, also kills herself, not wishing to live without him. Their deaths end the quarrels of the Montagues and Capulets.'

Or you could tell a much longer story, beginning like this:

'Long ago in the Italian city of Verona lived two young people, Romeo and Juliet. They were the children of the city's two leading families, the Montagues and the Capulets . . .'

The story you tell depends on many things. Here are just a few:

- how much detail you wish to include (Rosaline? the musicians?)
- the audience for your re-telling (young children? examiners?)
- the style in which you tell it (factual? nursery tale? melodrama?)
- the reasons why you tell it (to inform? entertain? teach a moral?)
- how much of your imagination you use (to add extra scenes, or characters' secret thoughts, to Shakespeare's version).

Remember, there is not one single 'right' story. Every story is a re-telling, a different way of recounting what happens. Shakespeare used his imagination to create his own version of the story he had read. For example, Mercutio is almost entirely Shakespeare's invention, and Paris does not die in other versions.

## . . . but is *Romeo and Juliet* true?

There's no simple answer to that question. It all depends on what you mean by 'true'. In thirteenth-century Italy there certainly were two Italian families, the Montecchi and the Capelletti, locked in political struggle. But the Montecchi lived in Verona, and the Capelletti lived in Cremona, sixty miles away! No one knows whether the families had children called Romeo and Juliet.

The story of two young lovers from opposing families was very popular in Italy and France. Myths and folktales about them existed for hundreds of years before Shakespeare. He based his play on a poem published two years before he was born. That poem was an English translation of a French translation of an Italian version!

Although it's probably not true historically, *Romeo and Juliet* is 'true' in other ways, because it has lasted so long, and because people still find it fascinating, it has a truth in human experience. In every age, young people have fallen in love against their parents' wishes. Where families or societies are in conflict, troubles always lie in store for a boy and a girl from opposing camps who wish to marry. Poets, playwrights and novelists have been irresistibly drawn to write about the plight of such young lovers.

## Activities

To help you deepen your understanding of the story of *Romeo and Juliet*, try one or more of the following activities:

1 Write the story as:
   - either a mini-saga (in exactly fifty words)
   - or a fairy tale for young children
   - or a short modern novel set in today's times.

2 Collect re-tellings of the story from a theatre programme or from a book of Shakespeare's stories. Make a list of what's been left out of each. Write an evaluation of one version.

3 Make a list of the ways in which Shakespeare's play is different from any story about Romeo and Juliet.

4 Talk together about the ways in which *Romeo and Juliet* is true.

5 Find other examples of young lovers experiencing huge difficulties because of a clash between their families, cultures or societies.

# The oppositions of *Romeo and Juliet*

Oppositions and contrasts abound in *Romeo and Juliet*. The action begins with a violent clash between the feuding families. Throughout the play, divisions and conflicts beset the doomed lovers.

## Light and dark

The play is alive with images of light and darkness. The flash and sparkle of eyes, jewels, stars, fire, lightning, torches, exploding gunpowder, the sun and moon, are set against a darker world of night, clouds, smoke and the blackness of the tomb: 'More light and light, more dark and dark our woes!' Juliet, waiting for Romeo, aches for the sun to set 'and bring in cloudy night immediately'. Romeo sees Juliet's beauty flooding the darkness of the tomb with brilliance: 'Her beauty makes this vault a feasting presence full of light'.

## Fate and free will

At the very opening of the play we hear of Fate: 'a pair of star-crossed lovers'. The belief that Fate determines our lives echoes through the play. Romeo fears that Fate has unhappy things in store for him if he goes to Capulet's feast: 'my mind misgives some consequence yet hanging in the stars'. Juliet fears what inevitably lies ahead as she parts from Romeo: 'Methinks I see thee now, thou art so low/As one dead in the bottom of a tomb.' Romeo and Juliet struggle to break free of what Fate threatens in dreams and premonitions. 'Then I defy you, stars!' is Romeo's defiant challenge when he hears of Juliet's death.

## Love and hate

'Here's much to do with hate, but more with love'
The love of Romeo and Juliet is threatened by a society full of hate. Juliet fears for Romeo's safety at the hands of her kinsmen: 'If they do see thee, they will murder thee'. The hateful, hate-full, honour code that governs the feuding mafiosi of Verona will destroy Romeo and Juliet, Mercutio, Tybalt and Paris. Love, in Verona's masculine society, is about domination. The macho servants of Capulet joke about sex in violent, aggressive terms. The selflessness of Romeo and Juliet, equal in love, and willing to die for each other, is in strong contrast to the hate that fills Verona.

# Death and life

Death is never far away in the divided world of Verona. The old people brood over it: 'well, death's the end of all', 'we were born to die'. Young lives are abruptly cut short. Images of death pervade the language: 'death-marked', 'untimely death', 'death bed', 'canker death', 'cold death', 'death's darting eye', 'cruel death', 'detestable death', 'present death'. Death even becomes a person, shutting up the doors of life, eating the living, fighting on the battlefield. Most memorable of all is the vision that haunts the play, Death as Juliet's bridegroom: 'Death is my son-in-law, Death is my heir./My daughter he hath wedded.'

# Language and reality

'A rose by any other word would smell as sweet'
'What's in a name?' asks Juliet. It's Romeo she loves, and she would love him whatever his name. Shakespeare was intensely interested in the uneasy relationships between words (language) and what they described (experience, things, action, reality). In *Romeo and Juliet*, he shows how language (calling someone a Montague) creates prejudice and hatred. Tybalt is blinded by malice at the very sound of a Montague's voice when he overhears Romeo.

When Lady Capulet compares Paris to a book (1.3.82–93) or when Romeo early in the play uses the formal language of classical poetry (see page 212), Shakespeare exposes the differences between words and action, between feelings learned out of a book and emotions learned from genuine experience. *Romeo and Juliet* highlights the tension between words and action, between language and life.

# Public and private

The action of the play shifts from outdoor to indoor, from public to private spaces. In contrast to the violent happenings in Verona's city centre, and the grand occasion of the feast, there are quiet, intimate scenes in the moonlit orchard or in Juliet's bedroom in the Capulet mansion. The shift from public to private, from social spaces to personal meetings, is symbolic of other tensions in the play:

- the loyalties of groups (Montagues and Capulets) versus the loyalties of individuals towards each other (Romeo and Juliet)
- the freedoms of personal love versus the constraints of social life
- male dominance versus the vision of equality of the sexes seen in the love of Romeo and Juliet.

# Oppositions of time

## Past versus present

An insistent sense of time echoes through the play. Present time (the fast-moving events we see unfolding before us) is set against the background of a much longer history. We hear of an 'ancient grudge', showing the feud has been going on for years. The Nurse recalls Juliet's childhood: ''Tis since the earthquake now aleven years'. And Romeo imagines his life as a long sea voyage that ends in shipwreck.

## Youth versus age

The differences between old and young, between cautious, mature wisdom and youthful impetuous emotion are striking. Romeo's passion is evident: 'I stand on sudden haste'. The contrast with the Friar's advice is vivid as he urges 'love moderately, long love doth so'. But don't think the play is a simple contrast between youth and age. Juliet's father is given to mood swings and sudden outbursts as violent as any in the young people!

## Fast versus slow

'Wisely and slow, they stumble that run fast', advises Friar Lawrence. It's not just the contrast between passion and caution that we've just seen in 'youth versus age'. There are changes in tempo throughout the play. In Capulet's orchard time seems to stand still as Romeo and Juliet exchange vows of love.

After leisurely beginnings, scenes explode into violent action. Events force the lovers into hasty action. Capulet's decision to bring the wedding forward hurries Juliet into drinking the Friar's potion. News of her 'death' sends Romeo speeding back to Verona.

## Dream time versus real time

'Dreamers often lie'

Dream time is quite different from normal time. What happens in dream time may or may not be true. Romeo wants to believe what happens in dream time: 'my dreams presage some joyful news at hand'. But premonitions are like baleful day-dreams, and those of Romeo and Juliet are full of ominous foreboding as future events come crowding into the present.

# Characters – who's who in
## *Romeo and Juliet*

The cast list on page 1 names the characters in the play. But what are they like? The following activities will help you develop your insights into character.

1 Collect examples of a character's language.
   Follow a character through the play. Collect lines that you think are typical of him or her. What do those lines tell you about the character? Which six words best describe him or her?

2 Collect examples of a character's actions.
   Actions, as much as words, are very revealing of character. Make a list of what your character actually does throughout the play.

3 Collect 'casting photographs'.
   From magazines or newspapers, cut out and display photographs of people who look like characters in the play. What do you see in each face that makes you think of a particular character? But remember what Shakespeare wrote in *Macbeth*: 'there's no art to find the mind's construction in the face'. You can't tell what people are really like from how they look!

4 Explore a character's motives in one of the following ways:

- 'Hot seating' – one person steps into the role of the character. Group members ask questions of the 'why did you do this?' type.
- 'Psychiatrist's couch' – one person becomes the character and is psychoanalysed by a partner or other members of the group.
- 'Select committee' – the character is interviewed about his or her actions by a parliamentary select committee.
- 'Chat show' – the character appears on a popular television talk show and is questioned by the host.
- 'Autobiography' – imagine yourself as the character. Write your life story.
- 'Biography' – write a biography of a character. Remember, a biographer's own point of view is important. Biographies of Romeo written by Juliet, or Tybalt or Benvolio would be very different.

5 See a production of the play!
   Does each character look and act as you expected?

# Why did Romeo and Juliet die?

Who's to blame? For hundreds of years people have argued over the reason for the deaths of the young lovers. Why not conduct your own enquiry into the causes of the tragedy? You can investigate in many ways: through mock trials or select committees, or by using the techniques of investigative journalism or television.

Call witnesses (including those who do not speak in the play, e.g. 'the lively Helena' or Petruchio). Require characters to defend themselves against the charge of being guilty of causing the deaths. Invent other characters who might also have something to contribute: a householder whose window overlooks Verona's public square; a boy who had crept into Capulet's orchard to steal fruit.

Don't simply try to pin blame on particular individuals. Seek other reasons for the tragedy. Here are suggestions you can use to investigate what caused the deaths of Romeo and Juliet.

## 1 Was it fate?

Were the deaths foretold in the stars? There are many suggestions in the play that the deaths were determined by fate. Collect references to the inevitability of the tragedy, e.g. 'star-crossed' (Prologue, line 6), 'the yoke of inauspicious stars' (5.3.111). Use modern horoscopes as evidence. You might even call on an astrologer!

## 2 Was it chance?

Was it just bad luck? Fortune is fickle, so maybe no one is responsible, only a series of accidents. Collect examples of chance and accident ('misadventured piteous overthrows'), e.g. the accidental meeting of Peter, carrying Capulet's invitation list, with Benvolio and Romeo; the non-delivery of Friar Lawrence's letter. Was Mercutio's death just an unhappy chance happening?

## 3 Was it adolescent passion?

Some critics have laid the blame on the folly of Romeo and Juliet in their youthful haste and passion. But how far do you think it was the lovers' own fault? Is adolescent love at first sight a cause of the tragedy? Collect examples of haste and passion in the play to use as evidence.

## 4 Was it the feud?

Were the deaths caused by the enmity of the Montagues and Capulets? The two families struggle for power in Verona. Their 'ancient grudge' breaks 'to new mutiny' at the start of the play. A stiff-necked code of honour makes the young men spring to violent, bloody action. Tybalt feels that 'the honour of my kin' has been insulted by Romeo's presence at Capulet's feast. Romeo is provoked into 'fire-eyed fury' by the death of Mercutio. He embraces the revenge code that governs relationships between the two rival factions of the Verona mafiosi. Collect other examples suggesting the lovers' deaths are caused by the quarrel that fractures the city.

## 5 Was it fathers?

Verona is a patriarchal city. Fathers hold virtually absolute sway over their daughters. They may give them to whoever they choose, and feel deeply insulted if their daughters dare choose otherwise. Juliet makes that choice and incurs the unmitigated wrath of Capulet:

'. . . go with Paris to Saint Peter's Church
Or I will drag thee on a hurdle thither' (3.5.154–5).

Together with patriarchy goes all the machismo of the young men. They relish crude sexual joking, see love as brutal conquest, and have no understanding of gentler, equal relations between the sexes.

Collect other examples that help you enquire into whether Verona's male-dominated society is responsible for the lovers' deaths.

## 6 What other causes?

- Is the tragedy caused by love itself? Their love makes Romeo and Juliet feel that meeting in death is the only worthwhile ending. 'Well, Juliet, I will lie with thee tonight' (5.1.34) is Romeo's expression of that love in death.
- Should you question the Friar's motives? He marries the lovers in secret, then devises dangerous plans that will ensure his own part in the affair is concealed. Juliet fears that he might have given her a real poison 'lest in this marriage he should be dishonoured' (4.3.26).
- Or might the cause lie in the 'rude will' of human nature? The Friar sees such self-centredness resulting in evil if it gains the upper hand over 'grace' (2.3.27–30).

Seek out more reasons of your own for the tragedy. Like everything to do with Shakespeare, it will be very unusual to find a single cause!

# The language of *Romeo and Juliet*

Shakespeare was fascinated by language. He couldn't resist playing with words, rhythms and styles. He loved to invent words, and to give existing words new meanings by fresh uses and unexpected twists.

## Listen! It's all around you!

Shakespeare's language is still very much in use, but we just don't notice it because it's so familiar. Here are just some expressions from *Romeo and Juliet* you can hear today. Listen out for them!

| | |
|---|---|
| star-crossed lovers | if love be blind |
| parting is such sweet sorrow | as true as steel |
| above compare | cock-a-hoop |
| light of heart | as gentle as a lamb |
| in a fool's paradise | past help |
| what's in a name? | on a wild goose chase |
| what must be shall be | we were born to die |
| I will not budge | stiff and stark |
| where have you been gadding? | on pain of death |
| let me alone | the weakest go to the wall |
| fortune's fool | go like lightning |
| a rose by any other word | a plague on both your houses |
|   would smell as sweet | where the devil? |

Use these familiar expressions to make up a short story. Include other familiar sayings you find in *Romeo and Juliet*.

## Creating atmosphere . . .

Shakespeare creates atmosphere by the use of words. Choose a favourite scene or part of a scene. Talk together about its atmosphere (aggressive, fearful, joking, etc.). Compile a 'language list' of phrases or lines that create the atmosphere. Use your list to make up a short play with your own invented plot and characters. Create as powerful an atmosphere as you can in your play by using Shakespeare's words.

## . . . and creating character

Choose two or three characters and compile a list of their 'typical' language.

## Sonnets

At about the same time as Shakespeare wrote *Romeo and Juliet*, he was probably writing his *Sonnets*. There are several sonnets in the play:

- Chorus at the start and end of Act 1
- Lady Capulet's praise of Paris (1.3.82–95)
- Romeo and Juliet's first meeting (1.5.92–105)
- their next four lines are the start of another sonnet.

A Shakespearean sonnet is a fourteen-line poem. Each line contains ten syllables. The sonnet has three quatrains (each of four lines) and a couplet. Or you could think of it in three sections:

- the first eight lines (rhyming ABAB CDCD)
- the next four lines (rhyming EFEF)
- a couplet (two lines) to finish (rhyming GG).

If that seems complicated, turn to the Prologue. Identify the rhymes (dignity/mutiny, scene/unclean, etc.) and match them with the rhyme scheme above. You'll find it is easier than it looks at first sight.

## Write your own sonnet

The quickest way to learn to write a sonnet is to have one in front of you and to write a parody of it. Turn to the Prologue and complete the following sonnet by carefully fitting the last twelve lines to the rhythm and rhyme scheme of Shakespeare's language:

> Two classrooms, quite unlike in atmosphere,
> In our school building, (where I write this down),

But of course it's best to make up your sonnet on a topic of your own choice!

## The sonnet tradition

The language of *Romeo and Juliet* shows the strong influence of the Italian poet Petrarch (1304–74). He became very popular with English poets in the time of Queen Elizabeth I. They drew on Petrarch's themes and style to write about courtly love.

In the play, Romeo's love for Rosaline echoes the major theme of Petrarch's poetry: a young man's unrequited love of an unattainable and disdainful woman. Romeo was infatuated with Rosaline, but she rejected all his advances. In 1.1.199–206, and 1.1.219–28 you can see the other influences of the sonnet tradition: neat rhyming; elaborate conceits (e.g. metaphors of war) and the word-play of wit, puns and repetition.

## The language of love and hate and fear and . . .

*Romeo and Juliet* is rich in many different uses of language. Here's a list of some of the kinds of language Shakespeare puts into the mouths of his characters:

| | | |
|---|---|---|
| love | hate | joy |
| cursing | mourning | anger |
| quarrelling | fear | command |
| praise | wonder | determination |
| urgency | joking | longing |
| rebuke | premonition | fantasy |
| taunting | nostalgia | straightforward explanation |
| quiet reflection | friendship | |

Find one or two lines that best illustrate each type of language. But remember that the language of love takes many different forms!

## What's an oxymoron?

'Loving hate' is an oxymoron because it contains two incongruous or contradictory words brought together to make a striking expression (e.g. 'cold fire'). 'Oxymoron' comes from two Greek words meaning 'sharp' and 'dull'.

Because so much of the play is about the clash of opposites (see pages 205–7), oxymorons are particularly appropriate to *Romeo and Juliet*. Romeo has a dozen at 1.1.167–72, and Juliet seven at 3.2.75–9. You can find practical activities on oxymorons on page 14.

## Metaphors and similes

Benvolio uses all the following as metaphors for swords: 'piercing steel', 'deadly point to point', 'cold death', 'fatal points' (3.1.143–66). But when he says 'they go like lightning', that's a simile. So metaphors and similes are comparisons. Different words, instead of the usual literal ones, are used to describe objects, events, persons and so on.

A simile uses 'like' or 'as' in the comparison, a metaphor does not. Check your understanding of metaphors and similes: which is which?

- 'shrieks like mandrakes' torn out of the earth'
- 'bloody Tybalt, yet but green in earth'.

Find five examples of each in the play. Also, listen carefully to other people's language. You'll hear hundreds of metaphors and similes!

# Repetition

Repeating words or phrases was a favourite and very effective device of Shakespeare. It might be a single word, such as 'civil' in the Prologue. Or it might be a line that adds depth to both drama and character. For example:

LADY CAPULET  The County Paris, at St Peter's Church
Shall happily make thee there a joyful bride.
JULIET  Now by St Peter's Church and Peter too,
He shall not make me there a joyful bride.

Such repetition increases the tightening tension of the plot and gives an additional insight into Juliet's character. Collect more examples of repetition in the play. Dramatise a few to show their effect.

# Puns – something to find out

A pun is a play on words where the same sound has different meanings. Shakespeare was fascinated by puns – especially in *Romeo and Juliet*. Mercutio revels in punning, often of a sexual nature. Even at the point of death he can't resist punning: 'Ask for me tomorrow, and you shall find me a grave man' (3.1.89–90).

But does every character in the play use puns? Discover the first pun each character uses. For example, Gregory and Sampson pun on colliers/choler/collar at the very start of 1.1.

# Shakespeare – and other writers' stories and language

Shakespeare almost always took the ideas for his plays from someone else's writing. He brilliantly transformed whatever he worked on. He found the idea for *Romeo and Juliet* in Arthur Brooke's poem *The Tragicall Historye of Romeus and Juliet*, written in 1562. But Brooke's long poem was pretty dull! Shakespeare's genius as a language craftsman made it powerfully vivid. Here are Brooke's lines about Juliet just before she drinks the potion:

'The force of her imagining, anon did wax so strong,
That she surmised she saw out of the hollow vault,
(A grisly thing to look upon) the carcase of Tybalt,
Right in the self same sort, that she few days before
Had seen him in his blood embroiled, to death eke wounded sore.'

Shakespeare concisely and memorably re-wrote Brooke's lines:

'Where bloody Tybalt, yet but green in earth,
Lies fest'ring in his shroud' (4.3.42–3).

# Putting on the play

There are an infinity of ways to perform *Romeo and Juliet*. No one way is 'right'. Every production is a fresh interpretation by the director, the actors – and the audience! But every production has its own particular 'space', usually a theatre stage. So let's have a look at Shakespeare's own theatre. How might *Romeo and Juliet* have been performed on the stage of the Globe in Shakespeare's time? Here's an artist's reconstruction of the Globe stage:

Take one of your favourite scenes from *Romeo and Juliet*. Make sketches showing how two or three incidents in that scene might take place on the Globe stage.

To help you, the pictures below shows one way in which the churchyard sequence of Act 5 Scene 3 might have been performed on the Globe stage. Identify all the characters shown, then sketch one further incident from the scene.

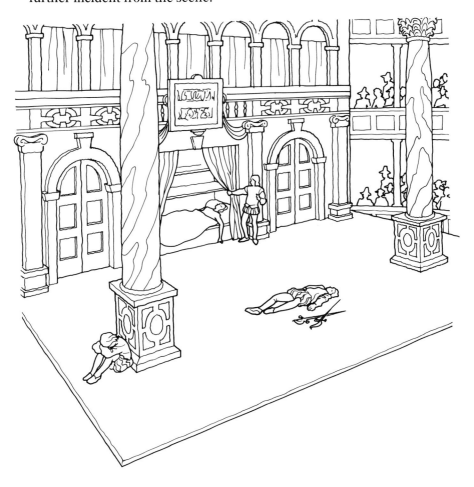

## Eighteenth-century stagings of *Romeo and Juliet*

In the eighteenth century, David Garrick's re-written version of *Romeo and Juliet* was very popular. He cut much of the dialogue, but added a funeral procession and a final conversation between Romeo and Juliet in the tomb. The play was acted in the fashionable costumes of the day as you can see in the picture.

Spranger Barry as Romeo and Miss Nossiter as Juliet, Covent Garden, 1753.

## Nineteenth-century stagings of *Romeo and Juliet*

In the nineteenth century, productions of *Romeo and Juliet* became obsessed with historical accuracy. Period costumes and settings were designed with meticulous attention to detail. Pick out features in the picture below which show attempts to recreate twelfth-century Verona on stage. Can you identify which lines in the play match the picture?

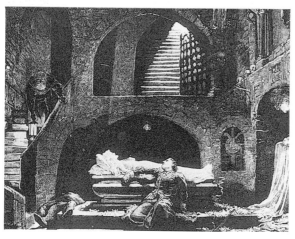

Henry Irving's 1882 production at the Lyceum.

## The twentieth century

The twentieth century has seen huge variety in the staging of *Romeo and Juliet*. But for all their differences, most productions have used a single basic set which can be quickly adapted to enable the play to flow from scene to scene. Modern productions are always concerned to avoid lengthy breaks for scene-shifting. Even though the locations shift from place to place, the flow of action is continuous.

Below is a photograph of the set for the Royal Shakespeare Company's 1986 production. Take scenes from different parts of the play, e.g. opening riot, balcony, Mercutio's death, Mantua, tomb. Talk together about how you would stage the action of each scene in this permanent set. Work out how each scene can flow swiftly into the next.

Royal Shakespeare Company, 1986. The basic set. What tells you that the scene is set in Friar Lawrence's cell?

## Stage your own production of *Romeo and Juliet*

Talk together about the period and place in which you will set your play: medieval Italy? modern Belfast? a South African township? a 'timeless' setting? Then choose one or more of the following activities. Your finished assignment can be a file of drawings, notes and suggestions, or an active presentation!

- Design the set – how can it be used for particular scenes?
- Design the costumes – look at past examples, but invent your own.
- Design the props – furnishings and hand props (swords, etc.).
- Design a lighting and sound programme – for one or two scenes.
- Design the publicity poster – make people want to see your play!
- Design a 'flyer' – a small handbill to advertise the production.
- Design the programme – layout? content? number of pages?
- Write character notes for actors' guidance.
- Work out a five-minute presentation to show to potential sponsors.

## Visit a production of *Romeo and Juliet*

Shakespeare wrote *Romeo and Juliet* to be acted, watched and enjoyed – not to be studied for examinations! So visit a live performance! Prepare for a school party visit through one or more of the following:

- Everyone chooses a character (or an incident or scene) to watch especially closely. Write down your expectations before you go. Report back to the class on how your expectations for 'your' character or scene were fulfilled or challenged.
- Choose your favourite line in the play. Listen carefully to how it is spoken. Does it add to your understanding?
- Your teacher will probably be able to provide one or two published reviews of the production. Talk together about whether you should read the reviews before or after you see the play for yourself. After the visit, discuss how far you agree or disagree with the reviews.
- Write your own review. Record your own perceptions of what you actually saw and heard – and your feelings about the production.

Two points to remember:

1 Preparation is always valuable, but too much preparation can kill the enjoyment of a theatre visit. So talk together with your teacher about how much preparation to do.
2 Every production is different. There's no such thing as a single right way to 'do' Shakespeare. But you might think that there are 'wrong' ways!

## *Romeo and Juliet* in five pictures!

Show your version of the play in five tableaux. Each 'frozen moment' must have a caption – in either Shakespeare's or your own language.

## Design a book jacket or cover

Study carefully the cover of this edition of *Romeo and Juliet*. Then design your own!

## Design a cast list

Have a close look at page 1, then design your own cast list. Make the relationships of the characters as clear as possible.

## Produce *The Verona Mail*

The class becomes a newspaper office – where time is always short. There are pressing deadlines! Your aim is to produce a full edition of *The Verona Mail* in two hours, using as much of Shakespeare's language as possible.

Choose a point in the play at which the paper will be produced. The class divides into pairs. Each pair takes responsibility for one or two sections of the paper, chosen from the following list:

| | | |
|---|---|---|
| news items | obituaries | advertisements |
| for sale and wanted | what's on? | weather |
| nature notes | food and drink | puzzle corner |
| cartoons | crossword | readers' letters |
| leading article | sports page | business pages |
| property for sale | travel pages | news in brief |
| international news | children's page | job vacancies |
| gossip column | science report | agony aunt |
| law report | horoscope | consumer page |
| births, marriages and deaths | reviews: films, books, plays | |

This activity works best in a two-hour session – or two separate sessions of one hour each. Work to the deadline! A tip: prepare for the two hours by looking through recent copies of local and national newspapers.

## Make your own video of a scene from *Romeo and Juliet*

Choose a scene or incident to act. Find a space somewhere in the school grounds, learn your lines, rehearse your scene – and shoot it!

# William Shakespeare 1564–1616

1564 Born Stratford-upon-Avon, eldest son of John and Mary Shakespeare.
1582 Married to Anne Hathaway of Shottery, near Stratford.
1583 Daughter, Susanna, born.
1585 Twins, son and daughter, Hamnet and Judith, born.
1592 First mention of Shakespeare in London. Robert Greene, another
playwright, described Shakespeare as 'an upstart crow beautified with
our feathers . . .'. Greene seems to have been jealous of Shakespeare.
He mocked Shakespeare's name, calling him 'the only Shake-scene in a
country' (presumably because Shakespeare was writing successful
plays).
1595 A shareholder in 'The Lord Chamberlain's Men', an acting company
that became extremely popular.
1596 Son Hamnet died, aged eleven.
Father, John, granted arms (acknowledged as a gentleman).
1597 Bought New Place, the grandest house in Stratford.
1598 Acted in Ben Jonson's *Every Man in His Humour*.
1599 Globe Theatre opens on Bankside. Performances in the open air.
1601 Father, John, dies.
1603 James I granted Shakespeare's company a royal patent: 'The Lord
Chamberlain's Men' became 'The King's Men' and played about
twelve performances each year at court.
1607 Daughter, Susanna, marries Dr John Hall.
1608 Mother, Mary, dies.
1609 'The King's Men' begin performing indoors at Blackfriars Theatre.
1610 Probably returned from London to live in Stratford.
1616 Daughter, Judith, marries Thomas Quiney.
Died. Buried in Holy Trinity Church, Stratford-upon-Avon.

## The plays and poems
(no one knows exactly when he wrote each play)

1589–1595 *The Two Gentlemen of Verona, The Taming of the Shrew, First, Second and
Third Parts of King Henry VI, Titus Andronicus, King Richard III, The
Comedy of Errors, Love's Labour's Lost, A Midsummer Night's Dream,
Romeo and Juliet, King Richard II* (and the long poems *Venus and Adonis*
and *The Rape of Lucrece*).

1596–1599 *King John, The Merchant of Venice, First and Second Parts of King Henry IV,
The Merry Wives of Windsor, Much Ado About Nothing, King Henry V,
Julius Caesar* (and probably the *Sonnets*).

1600–1605 *As You Like It, Hamlet, Twelfth Night, Troilus and Cressida, Measure for
Measure, Othello, All's Well That Ends Well, Timon of Athens, King Lear.*

1606–1611 *Macbeth, Antony and Cleopatra, Pericles, Coriolanus, The Winter's Tale,
Cymbeline, The Tempest.*

1613 *King Henry VIII, The Two Noble Kinsmen* (both probably with John
Fletcher)

1623 Shakespeare's plays published as a collection (now called the First
Folio).